Praise for *Women Make History*

"*Women Make History* is an illuminating and irreverent anthology, ranging widely over past and present. Replete with powerful stories, irresistible conversation starters, and beautiful illustrations, this book is a deep well of inspiration."

— **Stephanie Gorton,** award-winning author of *The Icon and the Idealist.*

"Sharon Spaulding has written an important book that documents the legacy of the heroic women on whose shoulders today's feminists stand. From warrior women such as Deborah Sampson, who fought as a soldier in the American Revolution, to the African-American poet Phyllis Wheatley, a "keeper of the soul," as Spaulding categorizes her, these women's stories show undaunted courage and vision. Each vignette tells a story, warts and all, of a woman who may have been forgotten but who accomplished the remarkable. This book will prove a vital tool for academics and writers, but also for today's everywoman looking for inspiration in our troubling times."

— **Trish MacEnulty,** author of *The Delafield & Malloy Investigations* mystery series.

"Sharon Spaulding presents brief biographies of women whose achievements should be included in our history books. A handful may already be, but many lesser-knowns are included here...These stories show how far we've come, but also raise questions about where we are now in terms of social, racial, or economic equality. Perfect for young adult readers on up, these biographies illuminate what we miss by not knowing about these extraordinary women and can serve as a springboard for discussion in schools, book clubs, and discussion groups of all ages."

— **Helen Frink,** author, Professor Emerita, Keene State College

WOMEN MAKE HISTORY

FIFTY-THREE STORIES OF COURAGE, STRENGTH & RESILIENCE

SHARON SPAULDING

Women Make History: *Fifty-Three Stories of Courage, Strength & Resilience*

First edition: February 2026

Illustrations by Carl Spaulding
Book design by Doug daSilva | dougdasilva.com

Published by Sharon Spaulding
An imprint of Outside the Box LLC

Library of Congress Control Number: Pending

ISBN: 979-8-9934369-0-6

Contents

To all those who were told they couldn't,
and did it anyway.

Dear Reader,

Back in the pre-internet days, I married one of Mary Ware Dennett's great-grandsons.

"Mary who?" you might ask, just as I did. Mary Ware Dennett *(page 89)*. She was one of the most pivotal leaders of the early women's rights movement. Mary's son, Carl, was in his eighties when my husband and I first visited him and his wife. They lived in a white Colonial house built in 1788 on a lake in New Hampshire. Mary's sketches and leatherwork hung on the walls and the books she owned and wrote lined the shelves.

Carl, my husband's grandfather, still had a charming, bad-boy mystique in his elder years. At night, after one too many gin martinis, he'd sit at the old, out-of-tune, upright piano and play honky-tonk music. When his fingers grew tired, he'd tell stories about what his mother had done to help women win the vote, and how she had taken on the U.S. government in the early twentieth century to legalize birth control.

Upstairs in the attic, under the eighteenth-century rafters where brown bats hung during the day, was an incredible treasure: steamer trunks filled with Mary's papers and journals. Each time my husband and I visited, I'd brave the bats and dip into those trunks. In her letters, made fragile with time, I came to discover her remarkable achievements, unrelenting courage, and sacrifices. I knew I wanted to tell her story and couldn't believe that beyond the Dennett clan, no one remembered her name.

After my kids were grown, I researched Mary's life and found mentions of other remarkable women whose names and stories were a mystery to me. I'd scribble them on notepads and stash them in drawers or pin them to my bulletin board, figuring that one day, I'd search for their stories, too.

In 2020, I was working on a manuscript about Mary when my book coach, Joey Garcia, suggested I write a newsletter about women like Mary—unsung heroes who had achieved so much, and yet, were mostly forgotten.

I began researching the names I had saved and soon had amassed a second treasure trove of history-making, life-changing, ground-breaking, courageous women—role models—whose stories deserved to be shared and passed down.

The first issue of my newsletter, *Women Make History: Stories We Should Have Learned in School,* was published in November 2020. With each successive issue, I fell in love with these powerhouse women and wanted to share their stories with as many people as possible. For that reason, I'm grateful you found this book.

The women whose lives you're about to enter have given me the courage to keep moving forward in situations where I nearly quit. I hope you'll experience a similar courage and strength that will propel you in meeting a new challenge or in moving forward with one you've already embraced. Imagine the kind of world we can create if we share these stories with our families, friends, neighbors, and co-workers. In short, with everyone.

— *Sharon Spaulding, August 2025*

ZITKÁLA-ŠÁ

DR. MARY WALKER

MARY ELLEN PLEASANT

The Warriors

SUE KUNITOMI EMBREY

ELIZABETH GURLEY FLYNN

DEBORAH SAMPSON

JOVITA IDAR

NINA ALLENDER

AN UNSTOPPABLE FIRE:

Zitkála-Šá

In the late nineteenth century, the prevailing political and social attitude towards Native Americans could be summed up in a phrase used by Captain Richard Henry Pratt: "Kill the Indian, save the man." Against this backdrop, Zitkála-Šá rose to become a powerful voice for Indigenous people. A fierce activist for Native American rights, Zitkála-Šá (baptized Gertrude Simmons Bonnin) wove music, writing, and political activism into her fight for equality and the celebration, not destruction, of Native cultures.

Born on a Sioux reservation in South Dakota in 1876, Zitkála-Šá liked to boast that it was the same year her tribe defeated General George Armstrong Custer at the Battle of Little Bighorn. Like many Native Americans, at the age of eight, she was sent to a Quaker school in Indiana for assimilation into white culture.

A quick learner, Zitkála-Šá was especially gifted in music and writing, but

"I was not wholly consciousof myself, but was more keenly alive to the fire within. It was as if I were the activity, and my hands and feet were only experiments for my spirit to work upon."

— ZITKÁLA-ŠÁ, *AMERICAN INDIAN STORIES*, 1921

her education came at a devastating price. Being forced to pray as a Quaker, speak only English, and cut her long hair ignited a lifelong struggle within her between the culture into which she was born and the culture in which she was educated. This struggle eventually became her motivation for speaking out on behalf of other Native Americans.

Scholarships enabled Zitkála-Šá to attend college and later pursue graduate studies at the New England Conservatory of Music. In 1902, she married a man who, like herself, was part-Sioux and part-white. In 1910, while working with the Ute tribe, Zitkála-Šá met composer William Hanson. They collaborated on *The Sun Dance*, the first opera about Native American life. Zitkála-Šá wrote the libretto and songs, basing them on sacred rituals that had been banned by the U.S. government. This marked the first opera co-authored by a Native American. *The Sun Dance* premiered in Utah in 1913, but when it was staged in New York in 1938, only Hanson was credited.

Zitkála-Šá also gathered, translated, and published several collections of Native children's stories. Her investigative journalism focused on the harsh realities facing Indigenous people and appeared in national magazines, including *Harper's* and *The Atlantic*. One article uncovered evidence that American companies gained access to oil by robbing and murdering Native people, particularly those from the Osage Nation. The article influenced Congress to pass the Indian Reorganization Act, which returned a portion of the stolen lands to the tribes and also granted self-governance. The conspiracy she uncovered is at the root of the best-selling book *Killers of the Flower Moon* by David Grann, and an Oscar-winning film of the same name.

In 1916, Zitkála-Šá moved to Washington, D.C., to devote herself to political activism. She helped to ensure the passage of the Indian Citizenship Act of 1924, which granted partial U.S. citizenship to Native Americans. However, the act denied people on reservations the right to vote in local and state elections. Unwilling to settle for less than a full victory, Zitkála-Šá co-founded the National Council of American Indians to repeal these laws. She served as its president until her death in 1938. The laws weren't struck down until the 1960s.

Zitkála-Šá is buried at Arlington National Cemetery with her husband, who had served in the U.S. Army. In 2024, the U.S. Mint issued a quarter with her likeness.

❧

BRING IT HOME: CONVERSATION STARTERS

Ask yourself: Would I be able to straddle two very different worlds that feared each other?

Ask a friend: Has your family shared stories of your ancestors dealing with two distinct cultures?

WOMAN OF HONOR:

Dr. Mary Walker

In an era when most women were denied access to a college education, Dr. Mary Walker had already broken barriers when she graduated as a surgeon from Syracuse Medical College in 1855. Ten years later, she made history as the first—and still the only—woman awarded the Medal of Honor for her courage during the Civil War.

According to the Congressional Medal of Honor Society, each recipient is a model of "intrepidity, above and beyond the call of duty, risk of life, selflessness, exemplary action, unwavering devotion, conspicuous gallantry, [and] extraordinary heroism."

Walker was born in Oswego, New York, in 1832, to a family that considered themselves progressive and believed in educating girls as well as boys. To enable their daughters to attend school, Walker's parents started their own. She then attended the Falley Seminary in Fulton, New York, and following graduation, Walker became a teacher. However, her dream was to be a doctor. Once she had saved enough money to pay for medical school, she applied to and was accepted at Syracuse Medical College. Walker earned her degree as an MD in 1855, becoming the second woman to do so after Dr. Elizabeth Blackwell.

Following graduation, Walker married another doctor but refused to take his last name, and she rewrote her marriage vows to exclude language about obeying her husband. Together, they started a private practice, but it failed, as most people weren't ready for a female doctor. The marriage also failed, and in 1861, when the Civil War broke out, Walker tried to enlist in the Union Army. When she was denied because of her gender, she offered her services as a volunteer.

> *"Let the generations know that women in uniform also guaranteed their freedom."*
>
> — DR. MARY WALKER, *HIT*, 1871

Even as a volunteer, Walker was only allowed to work as a nurse. As the war dragged on and casualties mounted, in 1863, the Army relented and hired her as a contract surgeon in the War Department in Tennessee. She was not recognized as an enlisted officer but was paid the equivalent of a lieutenant or captain.

One year later, Walker crossed enemy lines to help a Confederate doctor. When the surgery was complete, she was arrested by Confederate soldiers and imprisoned. Four months later, she was released in a prisoner exchange. There is speculation that Walker was a spy and that her capture was orchestrated to enable her to gather information for the Union Army. Shortly after her release, she returned to her position as a medical director at a hospital in Kentucky.

At the end of the war in 1865, Walker was awarded the Medal of Honor by President Andrew Johnson. In a stunning reversal, in 1917, the government rescinded the honor on the grounds that she had been a civilian and not a commissioned officer. Walker took great pride in the medal and refused to return it. She continued to wear it until she died two years later.

Throughout her life, Walker was a pioneering feminist, suffragist, and advocate for women's rights. In 1871, forty-nine years before women won the right to vote, she attempted to register to vote but was denied the opportunity. The same year, she also published her autobiography, *Hit*. In 1912 and 1914, she testified before Congress in support of women's suffrage.

From an early age, Walker advocated for what was known as the Bloomer costume, in which women wore trousers under a modified dress. Claiming it enabled physical mobility, she wore it throughout her wartime service. After the war, she abandoned dresses entirely and adopted trousers, a jacket, and her signature top hat. She was ridiculed and arrested several times for impersonating a man.

Walker died on February 21, 1919, and was buried wearing a man's black suit.

As of today, of the nearly 3,500 recipients of the Medal of Honor, Walker remains the only woman. In 1977, nearly sixty years after it was rescinded, President Jimmy Carter restored Walker's Medal of Honor.

In 1982, Walker was honored by the U.S. Post Office with a commemorative stamp, and in 2012, a bronze statue of her was erected at the Oswego Town Hall. In 2024, the U.S. Mint issued a quarter in Walker's image as part of its series recognizing women in American history.

∾

BRING IT HOME: CONVERSATION STARTERS

Ask yourself: Would I be willing to take a demotion
to work in the field I loved?

Ask a friend: Traditional marriage vows require a woman
to "obey" her spouse. How would you rewrite that vow?

MOTHER OF CALIFORNIA CIVIL RIGHTS & JOHN BROWN'S FUNDER:

Mary Ellen Pleasant

Mary Ellen Pleasant never learned to read or write, yet she became a notorious anti-slavery crusader, millionaire, and the secret funder of abolitionist John Brown's failed insurrection at Harpers Ferry in Virginia.

Born in Philadelphia in 1814 to parents of mixed race, Pleasant was known for her quick wit and street smarts. She also had a reputation for embellishing her life experiences when it suited her needs. In 1901, she dictated her autobiography to a journalist, but much of her history is undocumented or questionable because of conflicting narratives and, likely, because she was a woman of color.

As a child, Pleasant was sent by her parents to live as an indentured servant to a Quaker family on Nantucket. Determined to educate herself whenever and wherever she could, Pleasant became a clerk in the family store and learned the complexities of running a business. Like many Quakers, the family with whom

Pleasant lived were abolitionists. Through their connections, she was initiated into Nantucket's Anti-Slavery Society and became actively involved in helping enslaved people escape via the Underground Railroad.

As a young woman in the 1840s, Pleasant moved to Boston and became a tailor's assistant. She married James Smith, a wealthy mixed-race merchant who shared her anti-slavery conviction. According to fragments of a letter Pleasant wrote, her husband passed as white. He often wrote for the country's leading abolitionist paper, *The Liberator*, which brought the couple into the inner circles of the movement. The pair helped enslaved people escape to Canada, Nova Scotia, and Mexico.

Pleasant's husband died in 1848 and left her with an inheritance worth more than $1 million in today's dollars. She threw herself more boldly into anti-slavery work and began a partnership—or possibly a marriage—with a formerly enslaved man named John James Pleasant, whose last name she adopted.

Like Harriet Tubman, Pleasant risked her life by venturing onto Southern plantations to guide enslaved people to freedom. She adopted disguises, even masquerading as a jockey or stable boy to avoid suspicion. Eventually, her reputation made her a hunted woman. She fled first to New Orleans, then to San Francisco in 1852. There, Pleasant took a job cooking for a prominent family. She used her position to eavesdrop on conversations of the wealthy who came to dine and overheard stock tips and financial opportunities that she subsequently acted on.

Investing funds inherited from her first husband, Pleasant purchased restaurants, laundries, and homes throughout the city, creating a vast fortune. She also put her money to work in other ways. In 1859, the abolitionist John Brown was hanged for his attempt to start a slave insurrection at Harpers Ferry. An anonymous note in his pocket read: "The ax is laid at the foot of the tree. When the first blow is struck, there will be more money to help."

The identity of the person who had funded Brown's purchase of guns, ammunition, and horses remained a mystery until 1901. "Before I pass away," Pleasant said while dictating her autobiography, "I wish to clear the identity of the party who furnished John Brown with most of his money to start the fight at Harpers Ferry and who signed the letter found on him when he was arrested."

She admitted to donating $30,000 (about $900,000 in 2022 dollars).

During the Civil War, Pleasant assisted illegally enslaved Black individuals in California, a free state since 1850. She hid them in her own home and the homes of friends. Following the war, Pleasant used her fortune to help formerly enslaved people relocate to San Francisco and found them homes and jobs. Pleasant also aided young women trying to escape exploitative men in the rough, frontier atmosphere of San Francisco by helping them relocate and find work.

Pleasant's nickname, "Mother of California Civil Rights," resulted from two important legal cases. In 1863, she financed a lawsuit that gave Black men and women the right to have their testimonies heard in California courts. In 1866, Pleasant organized a sit-in of San Francisco streetcars because Black passengers were denied their use. She filed a lawsuit against the North Beach and Mission Railroad Co. and won. The decision was appealed but was later upheld by the California State Supreme Court in 1868.

Although her reputation as a philanthropist and entrepreneur earned her friends across many social circles, Pleasant was plagued by scandal later in life. Her ownership of several boarding houses attracted rumors that they were brothels for well-to-do men.

Another controversy erupted when Pleasant moved in with a wealthy couple to become their housekeeper. Gossip suggested that she was either the man's lover or a cunning thief extorting significant sums from her employer. When he fell to his death from an upstairs window, rumors erupted that Pleasant had murdered him. Charges were never brought, but at the age of 85, Pleasant was forced to move out of the estate, which she asserted belonged to her. In 1899, she declared bankruptcy, although *The Oakland Tribune* estimated her worth at $35,000 to $150,000 (approximately $1.4 million to $5.8 million in 2025).

Despite the controversy, Pleasant received an outpouring of get-well cards, flowers, and well-wishes from the community before she died in 1904. An article in *The San Francisco Examiner* said that her "deeds of charity are as numerous as the gray hairs on her proud old head."

In 1976, the African American Historical and Cultural Society created Memorial Park in San Francisco in Pleasant's honor. The park is on the site of her formerly disputed mansion. A ranch that she had purchased in Sonoma, Beltane, was designated a Black historical site by the National Park Service in 2021.

Pleasant is buried in Napa, and her gravesite is marked with a sculpture that was dedicated in 2011.

❧

BRING IT HOME: CONVERSATION STARTERS

Ask yourself: Would I risk my life repeatedly to help others, as Mary Ellen Pleasant did?

Ask a friend: What causes do you give monetary donations to on a regular basis?

AMERICAN CONCENTRATION CAMPS EXPOSED:

Sue Kunitomi Embrey

When the Japanese attacked Pearl Harbor in 1941, catapulting the U.S. into World War II, Japanese American Sue Kunitomi Embrey was eighteen years old. Within months, President Roosevelt ordered the evacuation of all Japanese Americans from the West Coast. Embrey and her family reported to a camp in the California desert called Manzanar. The experience ignited Embrey's lifelong passion for political and social activism. She became a teacher, author, and organizer to ensure that the sacrifices and stories of those in internment camps were never forgotten.

Born Sueko Kunitomi to Japanese immigrants in Los Angeles, Embrey graduated from high school in 1941 and postponed college to help her mother run the family business, a small grocery store. She was at work when news of Pearl Harbor was announced over the radio. The following year, Embrey's family had just six days to

"It's important to know about what happened because it could happen again. It might happen to another group of people or people with different political beliefs. And it's important for us to remember that we have a Constitution...and that is only good when people make use of it."

— SUE KUNITOMI EMBREY,
FROM A SPEECH

sell their business and dispose of all personal possessions before being transferred to Manzanar.

Two years later, Embrey was granted permission to leave. She moved alone to Wisconsin, where she had hoped to attend college, but she was denied admission to the University of Wisconsin on the grounds that a Japanese American would endanger war-related projects on campus.

When the war ended in 1945, Embrey returned to Los Angeles, and she married in 1950. She never gave up her dream of attending college. Nineteen years later, she earned her bachelor's degree, and, in 1972, her master's degree. She taught in Los Angeles public schools and advocated for inclusion of the history of Japanese American incarceration in grade school and college classrooms.

In 1969, twenty-six years after her incarceration, Embrey made her first pilgrimage to Manzanar. Of the 120,000 people sent to such camps, more than 60 percent were born in the U.S. and were citizens—just like her.

The next year Embrey co-founded the Manzanar Committee and eventually became its director. For the next thirty-six years, she organized an annual pilgrimage to Manzanar and also spearheaded efforts to have the camp declared a state and national historic landmark.

In 1972, Manzanar received the state recognition Embrey had fought to win. Sixteen years later, her efforts contributed to a congressional commission that declared the internment of Japanese Americans "unjust and motivated by racism rather than real military necessity." In 1992, Manzanar became a national historic landmark. Embrey then devoted herself to developing an interpretive history center at the camp, which opened in 2004.

Embrey also wrote *The Lost Years, 1942–1946*, a compilation of materials and interviews about Manzanar, and she coauthored *Manzanar Martyr: An Interview with Harry Y. Ueno*. She died in 2006 at age eighty-three.

❧

BRING IT HOME: CONVERSATION STARTERS

Ask yourself: How do I handle false accusations?

Ask a friend: Do you think racism still plays a role in false accusations?

REBEL GIRL:

Elizabeth Gurley Flynn

Although she died more than sixty years ago, the legacy of labor organizer, feminist, and civil rights activist Elizabeth Gurley Flynn is still hotly debated.

Born in 1890 in Concord, New Hampshire, Flynn was always on the side of marginalized workers, immigrants, and women. But her ironclad defense of the First Amendment and her hell-or-high-water approach cost her an education, her freedom, and her health.

Flynn was the daughter of an Irish immigrant and a miner who were both ardent socialists who encouraged her to join in their political activism. When she was ten, the family moved to the South Bronx, where Flynn attended public school and participated in socialist groups. Four years later, she had to leave school for six months because of an infection. It proved to be a turning point in her life. An avid reader, Flynn emerged from her illness at age fifteen as a devout feminist and socialist.

Soon after, Flynn gave her first political speech, "What Socialism Will Do for Women," in which she outlined the possibility of "industrializing all domestic tasks by collective kitchens, dining places, nurseries, laundries and the like." She also took to street corners, making speeches on behalf of the Industrial Workers of the World (IWW).

Flynn's ability to ignite crowds earned her the nickname "Red Flame" and also "Rebel Girl." Her oratory skills were so keen that her first arrest occurred because the crowd that had gathered to hear her speak spilled into the streets and blocked traffic in New York City's Theater District. Novelist Theodore Dreiser likened Flynn to Joan of Arc: "She electrified her audience with her eloquence, her youth, and loveliness."

Flynn was driven by two things: defending the First Amendment, which guarantees freedom of speech regardless of political or religious views, and equalizing the social and economic disparity that she witnessed around her. She later reflected: "I hated poverty. I was determined to do something about the bad conditions under which our family and all around us suffered."

Flynn's activism led to her expulsion from high school in 1907. Although this thwarted her intention of becoming a constitutional lawyer, it launched her into a full-time career with the IWW as a labor organizer. Alongside mostly male colleagues, she traveled across the country organizing unions and strikes for garment and restaurant workers, silk weavers, and miners. The demands were always the same: better and safer working conditions, higher wages, and shorter working hours.

On one of her trips, Flynn fell in love with a miner and fellow organizer, John Jones. They married in 1908 and had a son, but within two years, the marriage collapsed. In her autobiography, *Rebel Girl: An Autobiography, My First Life, 1906–1926*, Flynn said: "I romanticized the life—so different from New York—and the organizer who lived and worked there, under conditions of hardship."

Returning to New York and her family, who helped to care for her son, Flynn became more active in the battle for women's suffrage, reproductive rights, and equal wages. She joined Heterodoxy, a secret society of leading women activists.

When World War I began in 1914, Flynn joined efforts to prevent U.S. involvement. She was arrested under the newly created Espionage Act, which

> *"I fell in love with my country—its rivers, prairies, forests, mountains, cities, and people. No one can take my love of country away from me...It could be a paradise on earth if it belonged to the people, not to a small owning class."*
>
> — ELIZABETH GURLEY FLYNN,
> *I SPEAK MY OWN PIECE*, 1955

was commonly used as a political weapon to silence opponents of the war. The charges against Flynn were eventually dropped, but she then focused on defending others, mostly labor leaders and immigrants who were threatened with deportation for their pacifist views. These experiences led Flynn to cofound the American Civil Liberties Union (ACLU) in 1920. By the end of the decade, suffering from heart disease, exhaustion, and a failed relationship, Flynn stepped aside for much of the next ten years.

The economic collapse of the Great Depression pushed Flynn's views further left. By the late 1930s, when she returned to public life, she joined the Communist Party and became a columnist on feminist issues for *The Daily Worker*. Two years later, Flynn was elected to the party's U.S. committee.

At the time, America had a skeptical relationship with communism and the still young Soviet Union, but in 1939, when the Soviets signed a treaty with Nazi Germany, Communists became pariahs overnight. In what is still regarded as one of its most controversial decisions, the board of the ACLU booted Flynn and other Communist Party members from its ranks.

Flynn remained steadfast in her Communist views, but believing in political freedom, she supported America's entry into World War II. During the war, she advocated for equal pay for women and establishing daycare centers. Flynn also urged women to seek wartime jobs and to volunteer. She ran for Congress in 1942 as the representative from New York. She lost the election but won 50,000 votes. She also stumped for the re-election of President Franklin D. Roosevelt in 1944.

When the war ended in 1945, a renewed fear of communism spread across the U.S., and Flynn became ensnared in anti-Communist propaganda. In 1951, she was convicted of advocating for the overthrow of the government, charges she fiercely denied. Given a choice between prison or deportation to the Soviet Union, Flynn chose prison. She argued that her intention was to improve America, not desert it. She wrote about this in *The Alderson Story: My Life as a Political Prisoner*, and again in a second autobiography, *I Speak My Own Piece*.

Upon her release at age sixty-six, Flynn resumed her political activities. Although she had become critical of the Soviet Union, five years later, Flynn was named the first woman to lead the Communist Party of the United States. In 1964, she accepted an invitation to travel to Moscow. During her visit, she became ill and died. Flynn was honored by the Soviet government with a state funeral.

In his own autobiography, journalist Eugene Lyons described Flynn as "the most brilliant woman I had ever met. A veteran of the front trenches in the labor struggle since fifteen, she was, at thirty, attractive, winsomely Irish in her wit and her savor of life, with a remarkably cool intelligence behind her fiery oratory and personality...her eloquence and courage and sweetness...won her tens of thousands of worshipful friends among the workers."

Although Flynn has been the subject of several biographies and documentaries, her legacy still sparks debate. In the spring of 2023, Flynn's home state of New Hampshire erected a highway marker in her honor, and it quickly prompted an outcry. One politician, Joseph Kenney, remarked that Flynn was "a devout communist. We are the Live Free or Die State. How can we possibly promote her propaganda?" Others, however, expressed the view that Flynn was a figure of great historical significance and that it is important to understand the past.

༄

BRING IT HOME: CONVERSATION STARTERS

Ask yourself: What are my expectations of a true patriot?

Ask a friend: What issue is so vital that you would resist conforming, even when facing political pressure?

FIRST WOMAN IN THE ARMY:

Deborah Sampson

In 1782, Deborah Sampson disguised herself as a man and enlisted in the Continental Army. She fought for nearly two years in the Revolutionary War before her secret was discovered. Although other women did the same, Sampson was the first whose service was recognized by the government and the only one to receive a full pension.

One of seven children, Sampson was born in Plympton, Massachusetts, in 1760. When she was ten, her family sent her to work as an indentured servant to a large landowner. Eight years later, her debt paid, the self-taught Sampson worked as a teacher and a weaver.

As the Revolutionary War raged on, Sampson was determined to join the fight. She dressed as a man and enlisted in the Fourth Massachusetts Regiment under the alias Robert Shurtleff. Assigned to Captain George Webb's Company of Light

Infantry, she scouted territories to assess British troops and led raids on Tory strongholds. At the Battle of Yorktown, Sampson dug trenches and stormed a British fort as cannon fire rained down.

In one battle, she was shot in the shoulder and leg, and in another, she was grazed by a sword. Refusing medical help, she removed the bullets herself to keep her secret. However, when she later developed brain fever—a common ailment among soldiers—Sampson fell unconscious and was taken to a field hospital. The attending physician discovered her deception and informed her commanding officer.

The American Revolution

"...furnished no other

similar example of female

heroism, fidelity,

and courage..." than

Deborah Sampson.

— CONGRESSIONAL REPORT, 1837

While she recuperated, the two men maintained her charade. After her full recovery, Sampson was ordered to carry a letter to General George Washington, who granted her an honorable discharge. He is also reported to have given her money to cover her travel expenses home.

Following the war, Sampson married and had three children. On the advice of her friend Paul Revere, she spent a year lecturing throughout Massachusetts, New York, and Rhode Island about her exploits and often wore her full-dress uniform. Three years later, Congress approved Sampson's request for a soldier's pension at four dollars a month, about one hundred dollars in 2022 dollars.

Sampson died in 1827 at the age of sixty-six and is buried at Rock Ridge Cemetery in Sharon, Massachusetts. Her tombstone reads: "Deborah Sampson Gannett, Robert Shurtleff, The Female Soldier Service 1781–1783."

Four years after Sampson's death, her husband petitioned Congress for a military widow's pension. Although the couple was not married at the time of her service, the request was granted.

Sampson's story is recounted in early histories about American women, including Elizabeth F. Ellet's *The Women of the American Revolution*, published in 1848; Sarah Josepha Hale's *Mrs. Hale's Biography of Distinguished Women*, 1853; and Phebe A. Hanaford's *Daughters of America*, 1882. While there are conflicting accounts about Sampson, including the spelling of her name and her alias, one fact is undisputed: her courageous service during the Revolutionary War.

∽

BRING IT HOME: CONVERSATION STARTERS

Ask yourself: Would I risk my life for my country?

Ask a friend: Did you know that women disguised themselves as men to fight in the Revolutionary War? Would you ever do something like that?

STANDING HER GROUND FOR CIVIL RIGHTS:

JOVITA IDAR

Educator, journalist, and feminist Jovita Idar became a voice for Mexican American civil rights in the early twentieth century, especially for children and women. She also championed bilingual education as a means of preserving Mexican heritage and culture.

Born in Laredo, Texas, in 1885, Idar was the second of eight children. Her father was the editor and eventual owner of the progressive Spanish-language newspaper *La Crónica*, so Idar was exposed to political activism from an early age. The paper covered Mexican affairs in Texas and was a unifying force within the community.

After attending Methodist schools, Idar earned her teaching certificate in 1903. She then took a job at a school for Mexican American children in a small town. She quickly became frustrated by the school's lack of basic supplies and books, and she worried about her students who lived in extreme poverty and suffered from preventable illnesses. The stark inequities between white and non-white communities left a deep impression and changed the course of her life. Believing she could have a greater impact as a journalist, Idar left teaching to join her father and two brothers at the newspaper.

At *La Crónica*, Idar reported on racism against her community. Jim Crow laws (or Juan Crow, as some scholars refer to them) were in effect throughout the Southwest and targeted Mexican immigrants and Mexican Americans as well as African Americans. It was common to see signs posted in public places that read: "No Negroes, Mexicans, or dogs allowed." Extreme violence against minorities included lynchings, and Idar made it her mission to report on these horrific crimes. Perhaps as a counterpoint, she began to write poetry under the pen name A.V., which stood for "Ave Negra" or "Black Bird."

> *"Educate a woman, and you educate a family."*
>
> — JOVITA IDAR,
> FREQUENTLY QUOTED

When the Mexican Revolution began in 1910, Idar and her family became strong supporters of the insurgents fighting to overthrow Mexico's dictatorship. Aligned with the revolution's ideals of economic, social, and political equality, her family organized the First Mexican Congress in 1911 to focus on similar issues that confronted Mexican Americans. The Congress drew large crowds and featured women speakers advocating for women's suffrage.

To support the emerging feminist agenda, Idar formed La Liga Femenil Mexicanista (The League of Mexican Women), a political and charitable organization. Its efforts focused on educating Spanish-speaking children about their heritage and helping women achieve economic, social, and political parity. Idar was elected as the group's first president. Soon after, she launched *El Estudiante*, a bilingual newspaper for educators.

As the fighting continued in Mexico in 1913, Idar crossed the border to volunteer as a nurse with La Cruz Blanca, the Mexican equivalent of the Red Cross. She treated civilians and soldiers from both political factions.

Later that year, she returned to Texas and began writing for the newspaper *El Progreso*. In one article, she criticized President Woodrow Wilson for sending U.S. troops to the border. Idar's article angered both the Army and the Texas Rangers.

One day, under orders from the governor, Texas Rangers descended on the newspaper's offices intending to shut it down. Instead, they found Idar standing in the doorway, refusing to give them access. They left, but returned later to destroy the paper's printing presses, forcing the paper to close. When Idar's father died in 1914, she became editor of *La Crónica*. Two years later, she launched her own newspaper, *Evolución*.

Idar married in 1917 and moved to San Antonio. There, she started free kindergartens for Spanish-speaking children, organized political meetings, and worked as a translator. She also wrote for a Methodist Spanish-language newspaper, *El Heraldo Cristiano*. Idar never had children of her own, but she helped to raise her sister's children after her sister died in childbirth.

Idar died in 1946 at the age of sixty.

In recent years, Idar has begun to be recognized. Google honored her in 2020 with a "Google Doodle," and *The New York Times* published a belated obituary in its "Overlooked" series. In 2023, the U.S. Mint issued a coin with Idar's image as part of its American Women Quarters program. Increasingly, Idar is the subject of scholarly articles, biographies, and documentaries.

∽

BRING IT HOME: CONVERSATION STARTERS

Ask yourself: How can I be a better ally to those whose cultures are different from mine?

Ask a friend: Would we better appreciate our cultural history if we learned and spoke the language of our ancestors?

SHAPING A MOVEMENT:

Nina Allender

In the early twentieth century, with her sharp wit and artistic talent, Nina Evans Allender drew political cartoons that captured the news of the week and helped to shift public opinion of the women's suffrage movement.

Born in Kansas in 1872, Allender moved to Washington, D.C., with her family in 1881. From her earliest years, her dream was to be an artist. She studied painting at the Corcoran School of Art and the Pennsylvania Academy of the Fine Arts. From 1903 to 1907, she honed her skills under the mentorship of American Impressionist painters William Merritt Chase and Robert Henri.

Allender married in 1893 at the age of twenty, but it wasn't long before her husband left with another woman. It was rare for women to sue for divorce, but Allender did in 1905, and her request was granted that same year. To support herself and continue her artistic studies, she worked at the Treasury Department

"We shall fight for the things nearest our hearts. For democracy. For the right of those who submit to authority to have a voice in their own governments."

— NINA ALLENDER,
POLITICAL CARTOON, 1917

and then at the Government Land Office.

It is unclear when Allender joined the suffrage movement, but in 1912 she volunteered to help Alice Paul and the National American Woman Suffrage Association plan its groundbreaking march in Washington, D.C., to upstage the inauguration of President Woodrow Wilson, an anti-suffragist. Allender chaired two committees, one on "outdoor meetings" and another on "posters, postcards, and colors."

Soon after, she became president of the District of Columbia Woman Suffrage Association. A powerful orator, Allender regularly spoke at important suffrage events. But it was her political cartoons that most helped to win public sentiment to the cause of women's rights.

Although Allender considered herself to be a painter, political cartoons became her medium. From 1914 to 1927, her work appeared regularly in *The Suffragist*, a weekly journal about the movement, and later its successor publication, *Equal Rights*. In all, she contributed more than 150 drawings.

Allender's portrayal of women was radical for the era. To counter negative images promoted by anti-suffragists that depicted women as man-eating monsters, Allender portrayed them as confident, proud, and stylish. Posed with their hands on their hips, they appeared to look to the future, unafraid of their emerging political power.

During World War I, many suffragists picketed the White House day and night, holding placards that compared the president to Germany's Kaiser. When they were accused of treason and even jailed, Allender rendered the protestors as patriots, reminiscent of the Revolutionary War soldiers fighting for justice from tyranny. In addition to joining in the protests, Allender created the "Jailed for Freedom" pin—a badge of honor bestowed on women who had spent time behind bars.

After the passage of the Nineteenth Amendment in 1920, Allender remained an active member of the National Woman's Party. She continued to fight for women's rights and worked for passage of the Equal Rights Amendment. Allender retired in 1946, suffering from poor health.

In 1942, Allender moved to Chicago, then later to New Jersey. She died in 1957 at the age of eighty-three.

Before her death, Allender donated most of her original cartoons to the National Woman's Party. However, they were inadvertently placed in an unlabeled box and stored in a closet at The Sewall-Belmont House, the party's headquarters. In 2001, they were rediscovered. Today, the building is known as the Belmont-Paul Women's Equality National Monument, and in 2020, the museum hosted an extensive exhibit of Allender's work. In conjunction with the 100th anniversary of women's suffrage, Allender's cartoons were included in a variety of events, igniting awareness of her contributions.

The renewed interest in Allender has also brought criticism that she did not include women of color in her cartoons. Her critics argue that her work perpetuates the myth that suffrage was won through the exclusive efforts of women who were white and privileged.

∽

BRING IT HOME: CONVERSATION STARTERS

Ask yourself: When is humor a more effective strategy than debate?

Ask a friend: When viewing an artist's rendition of a historical event, do you assume that it's accurate or just the artist's way of seeing the world?

ELIZABETH MAGIE

EUNICE HUNTON CARTER

MARGARET IVES ABBOTT

The Game Changers

DR. SUSAN LA FLESCHE PICOTTE

ROSALIE BARROW EDGE

SERAPH YOUNG

SOCIAL ACTIVISM THROUGH ENTERTAINMENT:

Elizabeth Magie

In 1904, game designer, inventor, feminist, and economic activist Elizabeth "Lizzie" Magie created the board game later known as *Monopoly*. Whether writing short stories and poems, working as a newspaper reporter, or performing as a comedian and stage actor, Magie used social engagement and entertainment as a tool to bring about political and economic change.

Magie was born in 1866 in a small town in Illinois. Her father, a newspaper publisher, abolitionist, and economic reformer, encouraged his daughter's creative pursuits. One of his gifts to her—a copy of the book *Progress and Poverty*, by Henry George, made a lasting impression. She became a lifelong activist inspired by George's economic and social theory that individuals should own what they make or create, but that land should belong to the public.

Like George, Magie advocated for a single tax on land and the elimination of all other government taxes. She believed this would close the economic gap between wealthy landowners and the working poor.

As a young woman, Magie moved to Washington, D.C., where she worked as a stenographer and typist. Unable to support herself on a salary of less than ten dollars per week, Magie decided to draw attention to her plight and those of single women across the country. She purchased a newspaper ad offering to auction herself off to a husband. The stunt was social theater designed to spotlight the inequities between the sexes. It worked. The ad captured national attention from reporters and gossip columnists and also increased her name recognition and social currency.

"We are not machines.

Girls have minds, desires,

hopes, and ambition."

— ELIZABETH MAGIE,
PRESS STATEMENT

While working as a typist in 1892, Magie invented a mechanism that enabled a sheet of paper to run more easily through typewriter rollers. At the age of twenty-six, in an era when women held less than 1% of all patents, Magie received her first.

She received her second patent in 1904 for her invention, *The Landlord's Game*, the forerunner to *Monopoly*. The game had two sets of rules depending on how participants wanted to play. The first set had the goal of owning industries and creating monopolies by forcing others out of business. The second set of rules aimed to create collective prosperity by collaborating with opponents.

In a 1902 interview for the Georgist magazine, *The Single Tax Review*, Magie said of *Landlord*: "It is a practical demonstration of the present system of land-grabbing with all its usual outcomes and consequences. It might have been called the 'Game of Life,' as it contains all the elements of success and failure in the real world, and the object is the same as the human race in general seems to have, i.e., the accumulation of wealth."

In 1906, Magie moved to Chicago, where she co-founded the Economic Game Company to produce *The Landlord's Game*, but the company lacked the resources to mass-produce it. She later designed a humorous card game called *Mock Trial* that was published by Parker Brothers in 1910.

By the early 1920s, *Landlord* was popular among college students, some of whom made their own copies and variations. Magie's original patent on *Landlord* expired in 1921. To reassert control, she reapplied for her patent in 1924, and eight years later, Magie released a second edition.

In 1933, three decades after Magie had invented it, Parker Brothers published a version they called *Monopoly* and credited Charles Darrow as the inventor. Darrow later became known as the first American millionaire to make his fortune by creating board games. In a January 1936 interview with *The Washington Evening Star*, Magie stated that she had earned only $500 from her invention and received none of the credit.

Magie developed other games, including *Bargain Day* and *King's Men*, plus a third version of *Landlord* in 1939. In *Bargain Day*, shoppers compete against each other in a department store. Parker Brothers published two of these, but continued to give Darrow the credit for *Monopoly*.

Magie died in 1948 at the age of eighty-one.

Magie's legacy would have faded entirely had it not been for another game inventor, Ralph Anspach. In 1974, in his own legal battle with Parker Brothers, Anspach stumbled upon Magie's patents for *Monopoly*. Newspapers picked up the story.

Magie's contributions to American game culture also included popularizing a circular board, rather than the traditional linear form. She believed this shape facilitated social interaction, a novel idea at the time.

❧

BRING IT HOME: CONVERSATION STARTERS

Ask yourself: Have I ever taken credit for something I didn't do?
How can I make it right, even now?

Ask a friend: Has another person ever taken credit for your ideas or
work product? How can you protect your legacy in the future?

MASTERMIND OF A MOB TAKEDOWN:

EUNICE HUNTON CARTER

The granddaughter of enslaved people, Eunice Hunton Carter was the first Black woman in New York to become assistant district attorney. The only woman and person of color among an all-white team of special prosecutors, in 1936, Carter masterminded the takedown of the most powerful mob boss in history, the notorious Lucky Luciano.

Born in 1899 in Atlanta, Georgia, Carter grew up in a well-educated family of activists. Her parents held high-level positions with the National Association for the Advancement of Colored People (NAACP) and the YMCA. They were involved in the fight for racial and gender equality. In 1906, in what became known as the Atlanta Race Massacre, white mobs stormed into Black neighborhoods, killing dozens, wounding others, and setting fire to homes, businesses, and churches. The violence was so horrific that Carter's family fled north and settled in Brooklyn, New York.

The experience made a lasting impression on the young Carter. According to family lore, at the age of eight, she declared her life's mission to be "putting bad people in jail." An honor student, in 1917, she enrolled at Smith College and majored in government. Four years later, she completed both her undergraduate and master's degrees, becoming the second woman in the school's history to earn both degrees simultaneously. At Smith, she befriended Governor Calvin Coolidge, who became her mentor. Two years later, Coolidge was elected president of the United States. Throughout her life, Carter would count many political and civil rights leaders as friends, including First Lady Eleanor Roosevelt and Black activist Mary McLeod Bethune.

After college, Carter took a job in social work. She also married. She became active in the Pan-African Congress, a forerunner to the United Nations. The Congress regularly convened leaders from African nations to strategize about the peaceful liberation of their countries from colonial rule. The experience helped to shape Carter's view that issues of race, gender, and economic opportunity were global and that change could be brought about through legal and political action.

At the end of the 1920s, Carter enrolled in Fordham Law School. She graduated in 1932—the first African American woman to earn a law degree from Fordham. At the time, there were few female attorneys and Black women lawyers were almost nonexistent. Carter set up her practice in Harlem but struggled to find clients. Soon, however, New York City Mayor Fiorello LaGuardia appointed her as a prosecutor in what was known as "Women's Court," which dealt with prostitution and so-called "morals" cases.

Active in politics, Carter earned the Republican Party nomination for the state assembly in 1934. She campaigned on a platform of legal compliance for tenement housing and providing unemployment insurance for workers. She lost by just 1,600 votes.

The following year, Carter became the first Black woman to serve as assistant district attorney in the State of New York. She joined an elite team of nineteen white male lawyers who were then known as the "Twenty Against the Underworld."

Their mission was to end New York's organized crime syndicates, which had gained enormous power during Prohibition and the Great Depression. The mob was known for its brutality and violence, illegal gambling operations, supplying

> *"A country...which fails to allow its women to choose and develop their individual beings... thrusts away from itself a large part of the human resources which can give it strength and vitality."*
>
> — EUNICE HUNTON CARTER, SPEECH TO THE INTERNATIONAL COUNCIL OF WOMEN

bootleg liquor, and paying off judges, law enforcement, and politicians. The team focused its efforts on "Lucky" Luciano, who had united the biggest crime families under his leadership and was considered untouchable.

They set to work trying to connect Luciano to criminal activity, but he was insulated against prosecution. According to Carter's grandson and biographer, Stephen Carter, "While the nineteen white men...investigated corruption of the sort that made the front pages of the papers, Eunice was sent into the wilderness, consigned to what prosecutors of the era considered women's work."

Yet in that wilderness, Carter cracked the case. Drawing on her experience in the Women's Court, she pieced together a connection between prostitution rings and organized crime. At first, her boss dismissed her theory, but after several months of dead ends, Carter finally convinced him to reconsider the evidence she had amassed. This time, her boss approved wiretaps and raids on more than eighty brothels in the hope that a few of the women arrested might talk.

Carter conducted more than one hundred interviews herself and successfully connected three women to Luciano through the brothels. This became the key evidence at trial. In June 1936, Luciano was convicted and sentenced to thirty to fifty years in prison. Later, he was deported to Italy.

Although it had been her efforts that brought Luciano down, Carter was consigned to the role of courtroom observer and wasn't allowed to argue the case at trial. Yet her strategy earned her the nickname "Lady Racketbuster." In 1937, Carter was promoted to head the Special Sessions Bureau of New York County's criminal justice system, a department that handled 14,000 cases a year, making her one of the highest-paid Black lawyers in the country. In 1945, she returned to private practice.

Following the end of World War II, Carter was one of fifteen women invited to the founding session of the United Nations (UN). Two years later, she became a consultant to the UN, serving on economic, social, and legal councils. In 1955, she was elected to the highest position held by a woman at the UN, and in 1962, she joined its U.S. Committee for the UN Economic and Social Council.

Throughout her career, Carter traveled and lectured in support of racial justice. She was active in the National Council of Negro Women, the National Association of Women Lawyers, the New York Women's Bar Association, the YWCA, and the Harlem Lawyers Association.

Carter died from cancer on January 25, 1970.

Her legacy was all but forgotten until 2018, when her grandson and biographer Stephen L. Carter, a professor at Yale Law School, published *Invisible: The Forgotten Story of the Black Woman Lawyer Who Took Down America's Most Powerful Mobster*. She was also the inspiration behind a character in the HBO series *Boardwalk Empire*.

∾

BRING IT HOME: CONVERSATION STARTERS

Ask yourself: Do my actions fully express my belief in equality?

Ask a friend: What do you do when you know you're right but colleagues are dismissive?

GOLDEN GIRL:

Margaret Ives Abbott

In 1900, at the Summer Olympics in Paris, twenty-two-year-old golfer Margaret Ives Abbott became the first American woman to win Olympic gold. Although she continued to play amateur golf throughout her life and remained the reigning world champion until 2016, she died without knowing of her achievement.

Born in 1878 to a wealthy merchant family living in India, Abbott was a child when her father died unexpectedly. Her mother moved the family to Chicago, where Abbott's mother, an author, became the literary editor for the *Chicago Herald*.

At the time, women were barred from most sports. It was feared that rigorous physical activity would harm their reproductive organs and interfere with their ability to have children. In addition, corsets and other restrictive clothing limited a woman's ability to move freely. Golf, however, was considered acceptable for upper-class women, since it didn't require vigorous movement and women could

"Margaret Abbott possesses a natural talent for the game [and will become] one of the best women golfers in the United States."

— THE INTER-OCEAN NEWSPAPER, 1898

remain modestly dressed. Still, women had to have a male escort at golf clubs and on the course.

Family friend Charles Blair MacDonald introduced Abbott and her mother to the sport. MacDonald was the first U.S. Amateur Golf Champion and a renowned architect of golf courses. According to Abbott's biographer, Dr. Paula Welch, Abbott stood five feet, eleven inches tall, making her a natural who "could hit the long ball." Soon, she was competing in and winning local tournaments, and she had the low handicap of only two.

Accompanied by her mother, Abbott moved to Paris in 1899 to study art with Auguste Rodin and Edgar Degas. She continued to play golf.

In 1900, Paris served as the host city for the six-month-long World's Fair. The Olympic Games were included as one of the attractions, since this was only the second time in modern history that the games were held. According to historian Bill Mallon, Olympic events were regarded as a "sideshow" or an "afterthought" to the grander World's Fair. Olympic competitions took place over several months, without the festivities and fanfare that we associate with the Olympics today.

The novelty of the Olympics, the long span of time over which they were conducted, and the fact that they were a footnote to the World's Fair contributed to confusion about Abbott's gold medal. When she and other women entered the golf tournament, they believed they were participating in a World's Fair event, not the Olympics. The error was compounded by inaccurate reporting in the *Chicago Herald* about Abbott's win.

The 1900 Games also marked the first time that women were allowed to compete in the Olympics, and their participation was restricted to "ladylike" sports such as golf, tennis, and equestrian events.

Abbott's tournament took place on October 3, near Paris at the Compiègne Golf Club. Both she and her mother were among the ten American and French women who played. To this day, Abbott and her mother remain the only mother-daughter pair to have competed in the same event simultaneously.

Abbott scored a winning 47 on the nine-hole course, with driving distances ranging between 68 and 230 yards. Her mother scored a 65, tying for seventh place. Two other Americans, Polly Whittier and Daria Pratt, won the silver and bronze medals. After the 1900 Paris Games, women's golf was removed as an Olympic event until 2016, making Abbott the reigning champion for more than one hundred years.

In an interview after her win, Abbott attributed her victory to the fact that the French women wore high heels and tight skirts, which inhibited their ability to play well. Unlike the elaborate medals awarded today, her prize was an antique porcelain bowl. In 1902, she also won the French Femina Cup, the forerunner of the French Women's Championship.

Abbott returned to the U.S. in 1902, married, and settled into domestic life. She continued to play golf for personal enjoyment, but when she died in 1955 at the age of seventy-six, she was unaware that she had made history.

Abbott's story was unknown until the 1980s, when Paula Welch, then a student of sports history, noticed Abbott's name on a plaque at the U.S. Olympic Committee's headquarters. Welch inquired about Abbott but was unable to find additional information. She dug deeper and published her first article on Abbott in a 1982 issue of *The Olympian*. Welch continued her research and eventually located Abbott's son. He had no idea that his mother was the first American woman to win an Olympic gold medal.

Historians then began to reference Abbott's accomplishment. Her fame spread in 2018 when *The New York Times* included her in its "Overlooked" series. Five years later, Abbott was inducted into the Illinois Golf Hall of Fame. In 2024, when the Summer Games returned to Paris, news organizations picked up Abbott's story.

Abbott may have been unaware of her achievement, but her accomplishment opened doors for others. Since 1900, female athletes have consistently defied concerns about their physical and mental stamina. By the end of the 2024 Paris Olympics, American women had won twenty-six gold medals—57% of Team U.S.A.'s 126 medals.

BRING IT HOME: CONVERSATION STARTERS

Ask yourself: Have I done enough to seek out and celebrate the stories of accomplished women that history has forgotten?

Ask a friend: Why do you think there is so little information on women who have historically broken barriers and achieved at the highest levels?

MEDICINE WOMAN:

DR. SUSAN LA FLESCHE PICOTTE

Susan La Flesche Picotte was born on the wind-scorched prairie of Nebraska in 1865 during what would be the Omaha tribe's last buffalo hunt. The word "Omaha" means "against the current," and Picotte lived her life accordingly. Defying social and political norms, she became the first Native American physician in the U.S. and the first person to open a non-government hospital on tribal land.

Picotte grew up on the Omaha reservation in the crosshairs of time, straddling two distinct worlds: those of her tribe and those of the white settlers who governed their lives. Deeply concerned for his tribe's survival, Picotte's father, Chief Iron Eye, insisted that his children attend a missionary school to learn English and that they convert to Christianity. He even built and lived in a cabin instead of a tipi, in an area on the reservation some described as "the pretend white man's village."

But Picotte also embraced the Omaha way of life. As a young girl, she witnessed the death of a Native woman who had waited through the night for a white doctor. He never arrived. The experience haunted Picotte, and it became her motivation. "I saw the need of my people for a good physician."

In 1879, at age fourteen, she and her older sister boarded a train to travel more than one thousand miles to a school for young ladies in New Jersey. Two years later, she earned a scholarship to the Hampton School in Virginia (now Hampton University), which was founded to educate freed enslaved people and Native Americans. When she graduated, Picotte spoke fluent French, had a passion for music and art, and could quote Shakespeare.

But Picotte remembered the death she had witnessed and her father's admonition: "Do you...want to be simply called those Indians, or do you want to go to school and be somebody in the world?"

Picotte decided to become a doctor, but as a Native American woman, her ambition was next to impossible. Women couldn't vote, and they had few economic or educational opportunities. Women were also discouraged from attending medical school and were told that the stress would make them infertile. Some people even believed that women had smaller brains than men, thus making them less competent as doctors.

In addition, Native Americans were denied U.S. citizenship. When it came to what whites called the "Indian problem," the prevailing philosophy was assimilation through the complete annihilation of Indigenous cultures.

Yet, Picotte prevailed. When she was nineteen, she was accepted into the Woman's Medical College of Philadelphia. A group of wealthy, white feminists paid her tuition and mentored her. In return, she promised not to marry until after graduating and to work for two years as a doctor. Picotte completed her studies a year early and graduated valedictorian at the age of twenty-six. She returned to the reservation and became the only doctor for the more than 1,300 people living within the 1,200-square-mile tribal community. Smallpox, tuberculosis, and alcoholism were rampant.

Keeping her promise, Picotte waited until 1894 to marry. Afterwards, she continued to work, even after her two children were born. She was known to bundle them into her wagon to ride along on house calls.

Picotte's father had died before her return, and without a chief, the tribe often

> *"The Arrow of the*
>
> *Future Shot from*
>
> *the Bow of the Past."*
>
> — AS DESCRIBED BY A FRIEND OF
> DR. SUSAN LA FLESCHE PICOTTE

turned to her for advice on non-medical issues. In 1913, without government funding, Picotte raised the money and built the first hospital on the reservation. Its doors were open to all, regardless of race.

Picotte died in 1915 from bone cancer. She was fifty years old. At her funeral, three priests delivered eulogies in English, and a member of the Omaha tribe offered prayers in her Native language.

The hospital Picotte had founded served the community into the 1940s before it fell into disrepair. In 1989, the building was restored and renamed the Susan La Flesche Picotte Center. Today, it functions as a community center and houses artifacts from her life. It became a National Historic Landmark in 1993.

Picotte's story was mainly unknown beyond the Omaha tribe until the early 1990s, when Joe Starita published the first biography of her life, *A Warrior of the People*. In 2016, the documentary *Medicine Woman* was produced for the Public Broadcasting Service by Christine M. Lesiak and Princella P. Redcorn. The film chronicles Picotte's profound legacy and influence on Native women. In 2021, the City of Lincoln, Nebraska, erected a public statue in her honor.

෴

BRING IT HOME: CONVERSATION STARTERS

Ask yourself: What compels me to give freely of my time, talent, and skills to my neighbors?

Ask a friend: Have you ever felt like you had to straddle two worlds? What advice do you have?

THE CONSERVATIONIST:

ROSALIE BARROW EDGE

From 1929 until she died in 1962, Rosalie Barrow Edge used her wealth and invincible will to set the course for environmental activism in the twentieth century. Her visionary approach to wildlife conservation gave the world Hawk Mountain, the first sanctuary for birds of prey in the U.S., and also Kings Canyon National Park in California, Olympic National Park in Washington, and the addition of an old-growth forest of sugar pines to Yosemite National Park. Edge was also an unwavering suffragist.

Born in 1877 to a prominent family in New York City, Edge attended elite schools as a child and grew up in a world of social, cultural, and political privilege. She traveled the world and met her husband on a trip to England in 1909.

Despite her husband's objection to women's suffrage, Edge jumped into the movement in 1915 after the birth of her second child. She dedicated her considerable resources to passing the Nineteenth Amendment, and she joined the National American Woman Suffrage Association as Corresponding Secretary. She remained active in the campaign until women won the right to vote in 1920. The experience provided Edge with firsthand experience in grassroots organizing, running educational campaigns, managing protests, and understanding the nuances of political persuasion.

In 1924, Edge and her husband separated. She took comfort in taking long walks in Central Park, where she met amateur bird watchers and biologists from the American Museum of Natural History. Birding became her favorite pastime, and during her life, she logged more than eight hundred species in Central Park alone. She later described birding as "a solace in sorrow and loneliness."

It was on a trip to Paris in 1929 that Edge found what would become her life's work. Included in a bundle of mail from home was a pamphlet titled *A Crisis in Conservation*. It accused the highly regarded Audubon Society of corruption for secretly placing bounties on bald eagles, endorsing legislation that would allow wildlife refuges to become public shooting grounds, and catering to wealthy donors and sportsmen by negotiating hunting arrangements with developers and ranchers.

> *"...The most honest, unselfish, indomitable hellcat in the history of conservation."*
>
> — WILLARD VAN NAME, REFERRING TO ROSALIE BARROW EDGE, *NEW YORKER*, 1948

A member of the Audubon Society, Edge returned home to attend its annual meeting of directors. The Audubon president dismissed her concerns at the meeting. He referred to her as "the lady [who] had spoiled the meeting" because "her questions had taken up the time allotted to the showing of a new moving picture, and that lunch was getting cold." Edge was furious.

She launched the Emergency Conservation Committee (ECC) to "protect all species while they were common so that they did not become rare." Determined to inform all Audubon members of the organization's double standards, she sued the Society to obtain its mailing list and won. By 1934, the old guard of the Audubon Society was out.

The same year, Edge purchased 1,400 acres in the Appalachian Mountains of

Eastern Pennsylvania to stop an annual hunt of migrating birds of prey. She created the Hawk Mountain Sanctuary, which today encompasses 2,600 acres. Each year, an average of 20,000 eagles, hawks, and falcons migrate through Hawk Mountain.

Although Edge is most often associated with Hawk Mountain, she was also committed to enlarging national parks. Again, her efforts met with fierce resistance. In a brief biography of his mother, Peter Edge wrote that the National Parks and the U.S. Forest Service were allied with lumber interests and regarded conservation as a means of economic value.

Undeterred, in 1935, Edge and her son drove 13,000 miles around the country to visit most of the parks and to meet with local officials regarding projects she championed. Through her vast connections, she lobbied the secretary of the interior and indirectly, then-President Franklin D. Roosevelt. It paid off. Her efforts contributed to the expansion of Yosemite to include a forest of old-growth trees, as well as to the creation of Kings Canyon National Park and Olympic National Park in the state of Washington.

Edge remained a tireless conservationist until her death in 1962 at the age of eighty-five. Shortly before she died, she attended an Audubon gala unannounced. When her presence became known, she received a standing ovation.

Today, Edge is credited with instilling the grassroots approach common among conservation groups, including the Audubon Society. The Emergency Conservation Committee, which she founded, published more than one hundred essays and reports, as well as over one million copies of educational materials, news releases, and letters to the editor. It operated for twenty-two years after her death.

❧

BRING IT HOME: CONVERSATION STARTERS

Ask yourself: How do I respond when someone opposes me?

Ask a friend: What conservation efforts do you support?

FIRST AT THE BALLOT BOX:

Seraph Young

O n Valentine's Day in 1870, Seraph Young became the first woman in the U.S. to cast a ballot under equal suffrage laws. Two days earlier, the Utah Territory had unanimously passed legislation giving women the right to vote. Young, a twenty-three-year-old schoolteacher, voted in a Salt Lake City municipal election. Twenty-five other women also voted that day, and six months later, thousands of Utah women exercised their new political power. That power was short-lived, as Utah women's suffrage was rescinded by the federal government seventeen years later.

Little is known about Young other than that she was born in 1846 to a Mormon family in Nebraska, who moved to the Utah Territory the following year. She became a teacher and, in 1872, she married a Union Army veteran named Seth Ford. The couple had three children, two of whom survived, and they spent most of their married life

"...it's a typical example in history, right? That normal people doing normal things make history, or change the course of history, without even meaning to sometimes."

— KATHERINE KITTERMAN, HISTORIAN, *SALT LAKE TRIBUNE*, 2020

in New York and Maryland. Young's husband died in 1910. She died in 1938 and was buried next to him at Arlington Cemetery.

Although Young's ballot was the first, women's suffrage in Utah was complicated by the state's polygamist history. In 1847, Mormon pioneers found refuge in Utah, where they had moved to avoid persecution for practicing polygamy. The Utah Territory was repeatedly denied statehood because of it.

Initially, the federal government supported Utah women having the vote because Congress expected women to vote against the Mormon practice of having multiple wives. Instead, for the most part, Utah women voted as directed by their husbands and church leaders. Still, having the vote opened new doors. Church programs were created to educate women on political life, and some Utah suffragists joined the ranks of the national women's movement.

In 1887, Congress passed the Edmunds-Tucker Act, which intended to limit Mormon influence in the Territory. It rescinded women's voting rights. Two years later, the Church disavowed polygamy and, in 1896, Utah was admitted to the Union as a state. Women's voting rights were reinstated.

Young's legacy would have been forgotten were it not for local newspapers covering the groundbreaking event and listing her name. Today, Young is memorialized by a mural at the Utah State Capitol in the North House Chamber. It was painted in 2007 by David Koch.

⁂

BRING IT HOME: CONVERSATION STARTERS

Ask yourself: Have I ever felt my vote didn't matter?

Ask a friend: What can women do better to ensure their votes and their opinions count?

MARGARET CRANE

MAGGIE LENA WALKER

MARJORIE MERRIWEATHER POST

The Empire Builders

MADAM C.J. WALKER

ALICE GUY-BLACHÉ

JULIA DEFOREST TUTTLE

INDUSTRY FOUNDER WHO RECEIVED NO PROFITS:

Margaret Crane

In 1967, when twenty-six-year-old graphic designer Margaret Crane took a job with a pharmaceutical giant outside New York, she never imagined that her most significant contribution to the company—and women worldwide—would be a scientific invention. Using a paperclip holder, reflective Mylar, a test tube, and an eyedropper, Crane developed the prototype for the first at-home pregnancy test and launched a multimillion-dollar industry.

Born in 1941, "Meg" Crane was hired to design packaging and other promotional items for the Organon pharmaceutical company in New Jersey. In one of the labs, Crane noticed "rows of test tubes with mirrors underneath them" and was told they were pregnancy tests. In the 1960s, pregnancy tests were only administered by doctors in their offices and then sent to labs for processing. The procedure involved adding a few drops of a woman's urine to a chemical solution, shaking it, then leaving it to sit for a few hours. The solution turned a specific color if the result was positive.

It seemed so simple to Crane that she wondered why women couldn't perform it themselves in the privacy of their own homes. According to Crane, she replicated the testing device by using a plastic paperclip box and lining the bottom with reflective Mylar. She added a test tube and an eyedropper and presented her prototype at work, where it met with firm resistance.

"Every Woman Has the Right to Know Whether or Not She Is Pregnant."

— MARGARET CRANE, AD FOR A HOME PREGNANCY TEST

Crane recalls, "They said women should not know this [information] for themselves...It would be used for abortions, someone would kill herself, and the company would be sued." Organon was afraid of political and social repercussions and losing lucrative business from doctors, who held the monopoly on administering pregnancy tests.

Although the sexual revolution was underway, in 1967, it was illegal in twenty-six states for doctors to prescribe contraception to unmarried women. To obtain birth control, single women often had to lie about their marital status, wear fake wedding rings, and provide other false information.

Soon after Crane's idea was rejected, Organon began developing similar prototypes. When Crane discovered that the company had hired an advertising agency to determine the product's market potential, she sneaked into the meeting and placed her design alongside the others. The marketing expert selected Crane's prototype as the one with the greatest consumer appeal. Organon filed for a patent and listed Crane as its inventor.

Named the Predictor, Crane's test kit was initially marketed in Canada, but it took nearly ten years to receive FDA approval in the U.S. Today, at-home pregnancy tests are used by women around the world, and it is estimated that eight out of ten women administer the test themselves.

Although Crane launched a multimillion-dollar industry, she never benefited from it financially. For the sum of one dollar, she signed over the rights to her design. She never received the dollar. Organon licensed the product to three other pharmaceutical companies.

Crane's groundbreaking contribution would have remained unknown, but in

2012, Pagan Kennedy of *The New York Times* wrote a piece about the history of home pregnancy tests. Crane read the article, and when she saw that her name was missing, she reached out to Kennedy, who wrote a subsequent piece. Since then, Crane is beginning to be recognized for her invention.

According to Kennedy, Crane "...understood what an at-home pregnancy test would mean: It was a way for a woman to peer into her own body and to make her own decisions about it, without anyone else—husband, boyfriend, boss, doctor—getting in the way."

Crane also played an important role in marketing home pregnancy test kits. In that fateful meeting with the ad agency to explore the product's consumer appeal, she met the man who became her lifelong partner. Crane left her job at Organon, and the couple formed their own marketing company, Ponzi and Weill. Together, they created early advertising campaigns that helped to break down the social stigmas surrounding home pregnancy tests.

In 2016, the Smithsonian's National Museum of American History purchased the original prototype of the Predictor after it was auctioned at a price of $11,875.

As of 2025, Crane lives in New York City. Her partner passed away in 2008.

෩

BRING IT HOME: CONVERSATION STARTERS

Ask yourself: Would I lie if it meant I could get reproductive healthcare?

Ask a friend: Why do you think some people persist in believing that women can't be trusted to make decisions about their own bodies?

ENTERPRISE QUEEN:

MAGGIE LENA WALKER

Maggie Lena Walker was born into slavery in 1864 in Richmond, Virginia, the capital of the Confederacy. A brilliant entrepreneur, Walker became the first woman in the U.S. to start a bank and many other successful businesses. She was also a celebrated philanthropist and civil rights activist. Walker's business acumen brought her national fame, which she used to educate and empower African Americans, especially women.

After the Civil War, Walker's mother took in laundry and her father worked at a hotel, which enabled Walker to attend school. She excelled at math, but when her father died in 1876, the ten-year-old had to help support the family while continuing her education. Delivering laundry to her mother's wealthy white clients, she was troubled by the social, economic, and educational disparities she witnessed.

At the age of fourteen, she joined her local chapter of the Independent Order of

St. Luke, an African American fraternal organization dedicated to improving the social and financial lives of Black people. Walker took the mission to heart, and it became her life's work.

Graduating from the Richmond Colored Normal School in 1883, Walker took her first job teaching. Three years later, she married a wealthy brick mason, but a school policy against employing married women forced her to quit. Undaunted, Walker channeled her energy into St. Luke's philanthropic endeavors and began building community-based businesses.

In 1899, she became national chair of the Order of St. Luke. Against a backdrop of Jim Crow laws intended to dehumanize formerly enslaved people, St. Luke's teetered on the edge of bankruptcy. But Walker had a plan to make it thrive. Her approach was simple: bring people together by pooling resources. She said: "The pennies, dimes, and dollars of a thousand individuals change the weak word, 'few,' into the powerful word 'many.'"

Walker set a powerful example. Under the umbrella of the Order of St. Luke, she launched a series of businesses. In 1902, she began publishing the *St. Luke Herald* newspaper to build community pride and use as a vehicle to encourage African Americans to harness their economic power.

One year later, Walker became the first woman in the U.S. to apply for a bank charter and, soon after, she opened the St. Luke Penny Savings Bank. The bank quickly became a powerful symbol of racial pride. Ever the educator, Walker often handed out small piggy banks to children, a device intended to encourage young people to save their money. Each piggy bank held up to one hundred pennies, the sum needed to open an account.

To provide jobs for Black women and offer quality, less expensive products to the African American community, in 1905, she opened the St. Luke Emporium, a department store. Unlike stores owned by white merchants, the Emporium allowed Black people to try on clothes before they purchased, and it didn't charge them higher prices. The Emporium closed after a few years, in part because vendors refused to sell to the Black-owned store.

But Walker's other ventures were long-lived. She remained president of the Penny Savings Bank for nearly thirty years. By 1924, it had offices throughout Virginia and more than fifty thousand clients. When the Great Depression toppled the economy in 1930, Walker orchestrated the bank's merger with two other Black-owned banks and renamed it the Consolidated Bank & Trust. She became the new entity's chairman. As of 2025, Consolidated remains in operation and, according to its website, is "the oldest continuously operated African American-owned bank in the United States."

"When it comes to success, the choice is simple. You can... stand up and be counted, or lie down and be counted out."

— ATTRIBUTED TO MAGGIE LENA WALKER

Walker was a feminist who believed that the future lay in educating and empowering Black women. She held leadership positions with the National Association of Colored Women, served on the board of the Virginia Industrial School for Colored Girls, and held key roles with the National Association for the Advancement of Colored People (NAACP). A powerful orator, Walker was a frequent speaker at civic, business, and educational events in major cities across the country. A devout Christian, she often invoked biblical themes to inspire self-reliance and racial pride.

A strong civil rights activist unafraid to flex her financial muscle, in 1904, she helped to organize a boycott against Richmond's newly segregated streetcars. Urging others to "preserve their dignity by walking," she marshaled the resources of her newspaper and bank in calling for the creation of an alternative streetcar company. Within one year, the offending company failed, and a new one was formed.

Walker remained at the helm of the Order of St. Luke until her death in 1934. Under her aegis, it grew to include one hundred thousand members with chapters in twenty-four states.

Later in life, Walker suffered health issues from a long struggle with diabetes and, by 1928, she needed a wheelchair to get around. Rather than retreat, she remained an active public figure. She died from complications of diabetes. She was seventy years old.

Although she was largely unknown beyond the Black community in Richmond, the National Park Service helped to secure Walker's legacy when it purchased her home in 1979 and designated it a National Historic Site. Today, it serves as a museum and a tribute to her many contributions to Black enterprise. Located in the historic district of Richmond known as Jackson Ward, the area is regarded as "the birthplace of African American entrepreneurship." Walker once referred to Richmond as "...the Athens of the Negro race in America."

In 2023, novelist Ruth P. Watson published *A Right Worthy Woman,* loosely based on Walker's life.

<hr/>

BRING IT HOME: CONVERSATION STARTERS

Ask yourself: Have I ever demanded a friend's silence or denied their advancement?

Ask a friend: Do you think people define loyalty as silence or as toeing the line?

BUSINESS & PHILANTHROPIC GIANT:

MARJORIE MERRIWEATHER POST

When Marjorie Merriweather Post inherited $27 million in 1914 (about $850 million in 2025 dollars), she became the wealthiest woman in the world. During her lifetime, Post was renowned for her beauty, lavish lifestyle, and vast collections of art and jewelry. But she was also one of the most astute, pragmatic, and visionary business and philanthropic leaders in the first half of the twentieth century. When she died in 1973, she had grown her fortune into a net worth of about $2 billion dollars today.

The only child of cereal magnate Charles William Post, she was born in 1887 and grew up in Battle Creek, Michigan, when the family was still of modest means. She often helped to glue cereal boxes in the family barn. As she grew, so did the business. By age ten, she began attending company board meetings and visiting its factories with her father. Afterward, he would quiz her on the details.

According to her obituary published in *The New York Times*, when asked about the secret to her success, she replied, "My father." She also credited him with teaching her other essential skills, such as boxing. As a teen, Post regularly had to pass a lumberyard on her walk to school. Tired of catcalls and obscenities, she allegedly punched the worst offender and, from then on, was left alone.

When her father died in 1914, Post took charge of the family empire. She was twenty-seven. It would still be six years before women in the U.S. could vote.

"There are others better off than I am. The only difference is that I do more with mine. I put it to work."

— ATTRIBUTED TO MARJORIE MERRIWEATHER POST

A suffragist, Post became a member of the New York State Woman Suffrage Party, made large donations to the cause, and volunteered. In October 1917, she met with then-President Woodrow Wilson to lobby for the vote. Post kept her "Votes for Women" pin in her personal scrapbook until her death.

Post had married at age eighteen and had two children. She divorced in 1919 and then married Edward F. Hutton, a financier. Sharing a love for business, they began acquiring successful companies that could benefit from utilizing their existing distribution networks. Their first acquisition was Jell-O. Even as her wealth increased, at her lavish parties, Post regularly served her guests Jell-O and other products from her various companies.

According to Post biographer Estella Chung, when Post and her husband purchased Maxwell House Coffee and Sanka, she joked, "That nearly finished me off." Her father's first product had been a coffee substitute made from grains called Postum. "I had been raised with the idea that coffee was like taking dope so I nearly died at the thought of buying a coffee company and we paid $45 million for it." Other acquisitions included Hellmann's Mayonnaise and Baker's Chocolate.

In 1926, while aboard one of her yachts, Post's chef served a meal made from a goose that had been frozen for six months. In those days, fewer than half of U.S. households had refrigerators, but Post marveled that food could be frozen for such long periods and still be delicious. She became convinced that freezing meats, poultry, and vegetables would be the technology of the future.

Against her husband's advice, she met with Clarence Birdseye, the inventor of the process, and began a three-year negotiation to purchase his patents. Just before the stock market crash of 1929, she closed the deal and paid $20 million for Birdseye's operations. She also took her company public and renamed it General Foods. Her vision helped to catapult her company into one of the largest corporations in the world, but the power struggle with her husband ended her second marriage. She remained an active member of its board of directors until 1958 and was also the company's largest stockholder.

As a child, Post had learned that money was to be used for the benefit of others. She was known for making large donations, often anonymously, and taking an active leadership role in the organizations she supported.

During World War I, Post knitted and rolled bandages for the Navy. She also filled a transport ship with enough surgical dressings and equipment to outfit a hospital in France. When the ship sank, Post supplied a second one and built a U.S. field hospital that cared for more than 36,000 sick and wounded. After the war, the French government awarded her the Légion d'Honneur, the country's highest honor.

During the Great Depression, Post told reporters that those with means had "a duty . . . to prevent illness to our children who are undernourished." Under the auspices of the Salvation Army in New York, she opened a dining hall for women and children and funded it for six years. Wanting everyone to be treated with dignity and respect, Post made sure that its tables had clean and starched linens. In its first three months of operation, the dining hall served free meals to 120,000 women and 55,000 children. To finance it, Post put her jewelry in a vault and used the money she would have spent on insurance.

She also donated construction costs for the Boy Scouts of America headquarters in Washington, D.C. She provided the seed money for what became the John F. Kennedy Center for the Performing Arts, and she funded free concerts given by the National Symphony Orchestra. A supporter of education, Post became a house mother to one college fraternity and regularly invited "her boys" to her home for brunch.

Post built and managed several large estates, several of which she bequeathed to different institutions. These include Hillwood, in Washington, D.C., along with its furnishings, art, and jewelry collections, which she left to the Smithsonian. Her summer residence in the Adirondacks was bequeathed to C. W. Post College, named for her father. One of the most famous properties she built—the 17-acre Mar-a-Lago in Palm Beach, Florida—was given to the U.S. government to be used as a presidential retreat or guesthouse for foreign dignitaries.

At the time of her death in 1973 at age eighty-six, Post had been married and divorced four times and had three daughters. Her third husband had served as Ambassador to the Soviet Union in the 1930s, and during his tenure, she acquired a large collection of Russian and French art. It remains on exhibit to the public at Hillwood, another of her estates, which has been operated as a private museum since her death.

෨෩

BRING IT HOME: CONVERSATION STARTERS

Ask yourself: Did I pay attention when adults offered insight into the world of work?

Ask a friend: Do you believe that your money is for yourself or for easing the discomfort of others and making the world a better place?

SPINNING STRAW INTO GOLD:

MADAM C.J. WALKER

Madam C.J. Walker was born Sarah Breedlove in 1867 to parents who were formerly enslaved. She became the first African American millionaire, widely known and respected for her fortune, her political activism, philanthropy, and her unrelenting support of Black women. Her cosmetics company, which created products tailored to the needs of African Americans, is still in operation. Walker's hallmark was turning misfortunes into opportunities.

Orphaned at six, married at fourteen, Walker became a mother at eighteen and a widow at twenty. When her husband died, she moved with her daughter to St. Louis to be near her family.

Working long, grueling hours as a washerwoman earning less than $1 a day, Walker put herself through school by attending night classes. A scalp disorder, common among Black women at the time, caused her to lose most of her hair.

"I am a woman who came from the cotton fields of the South. From there, I was promoted to the washtub...[then] the cook kitchen...From there, I promoted myself into the business of manufacturing hair goods...I have built my own factory on my own ground."

— MADAME C.J. WALKER,
SPEECH TO THE NATIONAL
NEGRO BUSINESS LEAGUE, 1912

Determined to find the cause and a cure, she turned for advice to her brothers, who were barbers and knowledgeable about hair care.

Her scalp issues inspired her to take a job in 1904 selling hair products for Anne Malone, an African American woman who later became one of Walker's biggest competitors. While Walker developed skills as a door-to-door salesperson, she also began experimenting with her own formulas. She found that hair loss among Black women was partially due to poor diet and was related to products created by white-owned companies that lacked an understanding of African American needs. Eventually, Malone accused Walker of stealing trade secrets and fired her. Walker then launched her own hair care business.

Remarried in 1906, she took her husband's name and called her business "Madam C.J. Walker's." By 1917, she had hired and trained more than twenty thousand Black women nationwide as "beauty culturalists." The company also established programs to teach Black women how to budget and successfully build their own businesses.

As Walker's success grew, so did her philanthropy. Declaring that she "wanted the money not for herself, but for the good she could do with it," she funded scholarships for Black women to attend African American colleges. She supported other Black-run businesses and organizations, including the National Association for the Advancement of Colored People (NAACP). Walker also bankrolled the opening of YMCA chapters in Black communities and supported African American artists. As a political activist, she became a sought-after speaker and helped to organize anti-lynching protests and civil rights demonstrations.

Walker died in 1919 at the age of fifty-one, but her legacy lives on. In her will, she bequeathed nearly $100,000 to orphanages, institutions, and individuals, and also directed that two-thirds of future net profits be donated to charity. In 2006, Walker's life was the subject of a play by Regina Taylor, *The Dreams of Sarah Breedlove*. In 2016, cosmetics giant Sephora launched a partnership with Sundial Brands to produce products in Walker's honor. In 2020, Netflix produced a mini-series, *Self-Made*, about Walker's life.

∾

BRING IT HOME: CONVERSATION STARTERS

Ask yourself: Am I a glass-half-empty or a glass-half-full type of person? How has that shaped my life?

Ask a friend: When misfortune strikes those you care about, how do you respond to help them through?

BEHIND THE LENS:

ALICE GUY-BLACHÉ

A pioneer of the French and American movie industries, Alice Guy-Blaché was the first woman to direct or produce narrative films and the first and only woman to own a major studio.

Born near Paris in 1873, Alice Ida Antoinette Guy was twenty-one when she secured a position as secretary to Léon Ernest Gaumont, a renowned inventor, engineer, and industrialist. Soon after, Gaumont founded the world's first film studio. When Guy-Blaché volunteered to make a short promotional film to demonstrate the company's new motion-picture camera, Gaumont responded that, "It seems like a silly, girlish thing to do." He agreed, however, on the condition that her office work not "suffer."

Guy-Blaché had natural talent, and she became passionate about filmmaking. Soon, she was promoted to head of film production. In one of her films, *La Fée aux Choux* (*The Cabbage Fairy*), she portrayed a woman who selects babies from cabbages in a large patch. By the time she left the studio in 1907, she had directed, produced, or supervised nearly six hundred silent films, as well as another 150 movies synchronized with sound.

Guy-Blaché's early work is highly regarded for its energy and risk-taking. Preferring to make films on location rather than in a studio, she used twenty-five sets, outdoor venues, and a cast of three hundred extras in her thirty-minute movie, *La Vie du Christ* (*The Life of Christ*).

> "Alice Guy-Blaché is a
> fine example of what
> a woman can do if given
> a square chance in life."
> — THE MOVING PICTURE NEWS, 1911

Guy-Blaché also experimented with cinematic techniques. She developed the use of double exposures, blocking out sections of film and shooting over the same sections to add additional elements. In describing her influence, French professor Alan Williams remarked that Guy-Blaché "created and nurtured the mood of excitement and sheer aesthetic pleasure." Her biographer, Alison McMahan, noted Guy-Blaché's "focus on the psychological perspective of the central characters."

In 1907, Guy-Blaché married cameraman Herbert Blaché, and the couple immigrated to the U.S. Three years later, she established the financially and critically acclaimed film production company Solax in Flushing, New York. As company president, Guy-Blaché directed nearly fifty movies and supervised an additional three hundred productions. Success came quickly and, by 1912, Solax had outgrown its facilities. Guy-Blaché built a state-of-the-art facility in New Jersey for $100,000 and launched the careers of movie stars and production crew members.

Guy-Blaché produced melodramas, action films, Westerns, and comedies with social themes, including the concept of marriage as an equal partnership. In her action films, she often reversed male and female gender roles, casting women as the brave heroes.

The explosive growth of the film industry nationwide eventually forced the consolidation or closure of many independent studios, including Guy-Blaché's. In

1922, she declared bankruptcy. Her marriage failed, and she returned to France with her two children.

Unable to find work within the industry, Guy-Blaché lectured widely on filmmaking during the next thirty years. She wrote children's stories and published novelized film scripts. As time progressed, she discovered that many of her achievements had been forgotten or wrongly credited to male colleagues. Although she never made another movie, she worked hard to reclaim her legacy.

The French government awarded Guy-Blaché the Légion d'Honneur in 1953. Eleven years later, she returned to the U.S., where she wrote her memoir, *Autobiographie d'une Pionnière du Cinéma* (*The Memoirs of Alice Guy-Blaché*).

Guy-Blaché died in New Jersey in 1968 at the age of ninety-four. She is buried in a Catholic cemetery in Mahwah, New Jersey. Today, only a few of her hundreds of films survive. Her memoir was published posthumously in 1976, and a biography by Alison McMahan, *Wonder Shadows*, brought her back into the limelight in 2002.

In 2019, director Pamela B. Green produced the film *Be Natural: The Untold Story of Alice Guy-Blaché*, and the same year, *The New York Times* included her in its "Overlooked" series.

∽⁊

BRING IT HOME: CONVERSATION STARTERS

Ask yourself: How can I be an ally who ensures women get credit where credit is due?

Ask a friend: Has a male colleague ever been given credit for your work? What did you do—or wish you had done—in response?

MOTHER OF MIAMI:

Julia DeForest Tuttle

In the early 1890s, Julia DeForest Tuttle packed her belongings and left behind the comforts of Cleveland city life for the swampland of South Florida. An American businesswoman, visionary, and developer of what became the City of Miami, Tuttle is recognized as the only woman in the U.S. to found a major city.

Born in Cleveland, Ohio, in 1849, Tuttle married in 1868 at the age of nineteen and had two children. When her husband, an iron magnate, died ten years later and left her in debt, the resourceful Tuttle turned her home into a boarding house to pay the bills. But she needed more. Writing to her longtime friend and Cleveland native, John D. Rockefeller, Tuttle said, "I shall need to do something to increase my income... I have been thinking of getting something to do for a part of the year in a more genial climate... I could not do what would confine me constantly indoors or at a desk."

"It is... the dream of my life to see this wilderness turned into a prosperous country. Where this tangled mass of vine, brush, trees and rocks now are, to see homes with modern improvements surrounded by beautiful grassy lawns, flowers, shrubs and shade trees."

— JULIA DEFOREST TUTTLE,
LETTER TO A FRIEND

Tuttle was already thinking of South Florida, where she had visited her father, who had homesteaded an orange grove. In 1891, her father died and left his estate to her. The area, known as Fort Dallas, was named after an old military outpost. It was remote, rugged, and mostly uninhabited. But Tuttle jumped at the opportunity. She sold her house in Cleveland and arrived by barge in Biscayne Bay "with her adult children, furniture, and cows."

Convinced that a city located at the mouth of the Miami River and Biscayne Bay would become one of the greatest in the country, she envisioned it as "a center of trade with South America." With money from her parents' estate, she purchased 640 acres at the mouth of the river and also bought Fort Dallas. She renovated the building, made it her home, and it became one of the area's grandest estates.

Tuttle also built the first major lodging, Hotel Miami. Later, it was used to house workers who came to build the city. She is also credited with establishing the first laundry, bakery, and dairy there. But Tuttle knew that to build a strong economy, merchants, citrus growers, and tourists needed a railroad line. She launched an extensive campaign to convince railroad tycoon Henry Flagler to extend his train track to the area. To underwrite the costs, Tuttle offered to divide her real estate holdings with Flagler.

Tuttle's efforts were ignored until the Great Freeze of 1894–1895 devastated the orange crops of central and northern Florida, destroying fortunes overnight. The orange groves where Tuttle lived in the south were unharmed.

Although there is debate about the details, the story is that when the freeze hit, Tuttle picked fresh orange blossoms from her garden and sent them to Flagler. He finally gave in. As promised, Tuttle deeded land to Flagler to build the Royal Palm Hotel and also a railroad station.

On April 22, 1896, the Florida East Coast Railway line opened. Three months later, Tuttle, who was unable to vote because of her gender, watched as male residents voted to incorporate the new City of Miami. After its incorporation, Tuttle became one of the first directors of the Bank of Bay Biscayne. When customers complained that a woman was handling their money, Tuttle resigned.

Although she lived to see her dream realized, she didn't live long enough to witness a return on her significant investment. She died two years later, in 1898, from meningitis. She was forty-nine years old. With her untimely death and the large tracts of land she had deeded to Flagler, Tuttle left behind large debts, forcing her children to sell her remaining properties.

The Miami Commission on the Status of Women launched a campaign in 1996 to give Tuttle the recognition she deserved. A bronze statue in her likeness was erected fourteen years later, facing the seaport. It depicts Tuttle holding oranges and orange blossoms, and her skirt is embossed with scenes of early life in Miami and her vision for its future.

༄

BRING IT HOME: CONVERSATION STARTERS

Ask yourself: What would be the hardest thing for me to let go of when reaching for a dream?

Ask a friend: Could you push for a dream that was so big you might never see it come to fruition in your lifetime?

MARY WARE DENNETT

MARY MCLEOD BETHUNE

MINERVA HAMILTON HOYT

The Visionaries

DR. ELIZABETH BLACKWELL

MARY JANE COLTER

ANGELINA GRIMKÉ WELD

MARIA GUADALUPE EVANGELINA
DE LOPEZ

LUCIA TRUE AMES MEAD

SPEAKING OF SEX:

Mary Ware Dennett

Mary Ware Dennett was a pivotal leader of the women's rights movement in the early twentieth century. An officer of the National American Woman Suffrage Association (NAWSA), co-founder of the National Birth Control League and the Voluntary Parenthood Association, she was a leading activist for reproductive rights. In 1929, she was tried and convicted of obscenity for mailing a twenty-eight-page pamphlet, *The Sex Side of Life: An Explanation for Young People.* Overturned on appeal, her case set a landmark precedent that enabled the publication of James Joyce's *Ulysses* and other books previously banned in the U.S.

Born in 1872 in Worcester, Massachusetts, Dennett was the second of three children. Like her aunt, Lucia True Ames Mead, her family was dedicated to educating both girls and boys, and fighting for legal, social, and economic equality.

In 1877, when Dennett was five, the family moved to San Antonio, Texas.

A precocious child, her earliest known letters date to this period. In missives to her aunts in Boston, she complained that people in Texas said "howdy" instead of "hello" and "quit" instead of "stop." She also lamented that the school lacked art classes. When her father was diagnosed with terminal cancer, the family returned to Massachusetts in 1880. Dennett and her two siblings lived with extended family until her father died two years later. She resided with her two unmarried aunts and an uncle in Boston.

Feminists and brilliant scholars, Dennett's aunts took charge of her education. She studied Greek, Latin, German, mathematics, and public speaking. Later, when her uncle married an artist, the newest family member became Dennett's art tutor. Graduating with honors from the Boston Museum School in 1893, at the age of twenty-one, Dennett became professor of design at what is now Drexel University in Philadelphia. About this time, she met a like-minded architect, and they married in 1900. Three children followed, two of whom survived.

Dennett's happily ever after wasn't to be. She almost died in childbirth, and after her third child was born in 1905, she was told to abstain from sexual intercourse or risk certain death. At the time, federal obscenity statutes known as the Comstock Laws rendered all contraceptive information "lewd, lascivious, and obscene." It was illegal for doctors to discuss the prevention of conception with patients or, in some states, for parents to discuss it with their adult, married children. Anyone caught breaking the law could be arrested, imprisoned for five years, and fined up to $5,000. Many were.

Not long after her doctor's mandate, Dennett's husband took off with the wife of a client. When he asked Mary to form a commune with him and the other family, her response was, "Hell no!" She filed for divorce, got custody of her kids, and hung up her easel. She catapulted into the women's suffrage movement in Massachusetts and, in 1910, was recruited by NAWSA as a national officer.

Dennett moved to Manhattan, cut her hair and shed her corset, and, over the next four years, helped to organize campaigns that secured the vote for women in fourteen states. She also wrote the literature and communications pieces that became the movement's standard. But Dennett was haunted by the injustices of not having access to contraception.

In 1914, she met Margaret Sanger, who had started campaigning for reproductive freedom. Dennett had arrived at a similar conclusion: that true equality was possible only through access to information about contraception.

She left suffrage work and, in March 1915, co-founded the National Birth Control League. Its mission was to bring the topic of sex out from the shadows of Victorian morality and to change the Comstock Laws. Initially, as she had with suffrage, Dennett sought to change laws at the state level.

Also in 1915, she penned *The Sex Side of Life* as a way of speaking to her sons about sex. Three years later, she began mailing the booklet to anyone who requested a copy and paid her a quarter.

As for her relationship with Sanger, rather than allies, the two became bitter rivals for leadership of the burgeoning movement. Dennett believed in working through the system to bring about reform and couldn't abide Sanger's willingness to break the law or her publicity stunts designed to generate newspaper headlines.

> *"It seems a little stupid, this present method of teaching children that humans have bones, muscles, nerves, blood circulation, digestive and respiratory organs, and omitting the fact that they have sex organs as well."*
>
> — MARY WARE DENNETT

In 1918, Dennett launched a new organization, the Voluntary Parenthood League, to tackle reproductive rights at the federal level. She had realized that changing federal laws, rather than the state-by-state process, would be more efficient.

She drafted legislation and began to lobby Congress. It was a hard sell. Privately, most lawmakers supported the legalization of contraception, but publicly, they were afraid of taking a controversial position and losing re-election. A few chastised Dennett, telling her that she should be ashamed of her efforts and that having a large family "does 'em [women] good."

It was also in 1918 that the rift between Dennett and Sanger began to spill into public view. When Sanger declared a "birth strike"—calling for women to refuse to have children for five years—Dennett resigned her position on the editorial board of Sanger's paper, *The Birth Control Review*. Dennett was convinced Sanger's rhetoric would further alienate lawmakers. When Sanger launched the American

Birth Control League in 1921, she excluded Dennett.

By this time, the two women had very different approaches. Dennett believed that access to birth control should be available to everyone. Sanger thought that it should be accessible only through the medical establishment. Dennett struggled with fundraising while Sanger, an avowed socialist, married an elderly and wealthy industrialist who financed her organization.

In Congress, Dennett worked to find sponsors for her bill. Eventually, when it appeared that it had a chance of being brought to the floor for a vote, Sanger's crew allegedly spread rumors that Dennett was insane and that she lacked legitimate backing. By 1925, broke and defeated, Dennett passed the torch to Sanger and semi-retired to her work as an artist.

But Dennett had made powerful enemies including the postmaster general. In 1922, he declared *The Sex Side of Life* "obscene" under the Comstock Laws. She challenged the ban and attempted to persuade the American Civil Liberties Union (ACLU) to file suit against the government over the ban. Before they got the chance, in January 1929, Dennett was indicted. In April, she was tried and convicted. Her attorney, the legendary Morris Ernst, appealed the decision and, one year later, the verdict was overturned.

Although it wasn't the victory that Dennett had fought to achieve, the reversal of her conviction set a landmark precedent that began to undermine the Comstock Laws. Three years later, citing *United States v. Dennett*, Ernst successfully challenged the ban on James Joyce's *Ulysses*. The publication of several other books followed as the court's definition of obscenity began to change.

As the Great Depression settled in, Dennett's story faded from public awareness. When she died in 1947, her obituary in *The New York Times* neglected to include her work for reproductive rights. Dennett's papers were stored in the attic of an old family home until the early 1990s, when most were donated to the Schlesinger Library at Radcliffe College. In 1996, Constance Chen published the first biography about Dennett and, in 2025, Stephanie Gorton published *The Icon and the Idealist* about the Dennett-Sanger rivalry.

Until 1964, the Dennett family continued to sell *The Sex Side of Life* to anyone who requested a copy and enclosed a quarter. The Comstock Laws were not fully struck down until 1970. Today, some groups are trying to resurrect them.

∾

BRING IT HOME: CONVERSATION STARTERS

Ask yourself: When, if ever, do you believe it is justifiable
to break the law?

Ask a friend: If Mary Ware Dennett and Margaret Sanger
had joined forces, do you think women's reproductive
rights would still be at risk today?

BELOVED:

MARY McLEOD BETHUNE

Born in 1875 to formerly enslaved parents, Mary McLeod Bethune later became known as "The First Lady of the Struggle." She was a pioneering educator, civil rights activist, and advisor to five U.S. presidents who helped to shape government policy toward African Americans.

From an early age, Bethune worked alongside her seventeen siblings in the cotton fields of South Carolina. When a missionary school for African American children opened nearby, she enrolled and, at age ten, she became the first in her family to receive a formal education. She later noted that when she learned to read, "the whole world opened to me."

Walking several miles to school each day, Bethune was keenly aware of her family's plight and vowed to use her education to benefit all. At night, she instructed her family on what she had learned that day.

In 1888, Bethune earned a scholarship to a nearby seminary. After graduating five years later, she enrolled at the Moody Bible Institute in Chicago with the dream of being a missionary. Two years later, however, Bethune returned home to teach. She married a fellow teacher in 1898 and had one son. Soon after, they moved to Daytona, Florida, in search of better jobs.

Convinced that education was key to ending the cycle of poverty—especially among Black women—in 1904, Bethune founded the Daytona Normal and Industrial Institute for Girls with $1.50 as capital. The curriculum focused on teaching employment skills, including sewing and domestic science, agriculture, and teaching. Within two years, it grew from five students to more than 250. When Bethune's husband left her in 1907, she remained determined to keep the school operating.

Her finances were precarious, but she was resourceful. She wore hand-me-downs mended by her sewing students, and it was said that she scoured the garbage dumps in search of reusable supplies and made what she could. She whittled pencils from charred wood, made ink from pressed berries, and stuffed corn sacks with hay for mattresses.

But Bethune also became a convincing fundraiser. Her efforts drew the attention of Black and white philanthropists who vacationed in Florida. Many became donors, and some, including John D. Rockefeller, Jr., and cosmetics giant Madam C. J. Walker *(page 75)*, joined the board of directors.

Less than a decade later, Bethune added a high school. In 1912, to meet the need for medical care among African Americans and to provide job training, she established the Mary McLeod Hospital and Training School for Nurses.

As educational opportunities for Black women improved in the early 1920s, Bethune expanded her vision. She merged her school with the Cookman Institute for Men in Jacksonville and renamed it Cookman-Bethune College. She served as president until 1942. Under her leadership, it became a four-year college with six hundred students. Bethune's educational philosophy, "Enter to learn. Leave to serve," set the standard for other Black colleges. Now a university, the school remains in operation.

Bethune was also an early and outspoken critic of lynching and all forms of segregation. During World War I, while her son served in the Army, she mounted

"I leave you a thirst for education. Knowledge is the prime need of the hour."

— MARY MCLEOD BETHUNE,
LAST WILL & TESTAMENT, 1955

a successful campaign to have the Red Cross provide services for minorities in addition to white people.

Bethune always insisted on being treated with dignity and respect. When she was introduced as "Mary" at a Southern Conference on Human Welfare, she insisted on being called "Mrs. Bethune." It may seem like a small gesture today, but at the time in the deeply segregated South, it made a bold statement. Throughout her life, Bethune also joined picket lines to protest discrimination.

Bethune's influence expanded nationally. In 1935, she founded the National Council of Negro Women and served as president until 1949. She also served as vice president of the National Association for the Advancement of Colored People (NAACP) from 1940 to 1955.

Bethune became the first African American woman to serve on special councils under presidents Coolidge, Hoover, Roosevelt (FDR), and Truman. But it was her close friendship with First Lady Eleanor Roosevelt that helped her to bring race to the forefront of national public policy. In an era of Jim Crow segregation, Bethune and Roosevelt intentionally broke social taboos such as shaking hands in press photos, dining and attending events together. Behind the scenes, they worked to inform and influence President Roosevelt's policies on racial issues.

Under the Roosevelt administration, Bethune was appointed director of the Division of Negro Affairs for the National Youth Administration (NYA), making her the highest-ranking Black woman in the federal government at the time. At her urging, several Black men were appointed to leadership roles in FDR's New Deal projects. Bethune was also a member and the only woman in Roosevelt's "Black Cabinet," which advised him on African American issues.

During World War II, Bethune was assistant director of the Women's Army Corps. She used her position to advocate for the elimination of segregation within the defense industry and the military. When Black fighter pilots, who became known as the Tuskegee Airmen, were sidelined from combat because of racial bias, Bethune and Mrs. Roosevelt brought public attention to their plight, helping the legendary pilots to join the fight.

In 1942, Bethune left Bethune-Cookman College and moved to Washington, D.C. She took up residence at the National Council of Negro Women headquarters.

When the war ended, Bethune was appointed as a delegate to the conference that established the United Nations. In the early 1950s, President Truman asked her to serve on a national defense committee and also as an official representative to Liberia.

Bethune retired to Florida, where she penned her "Last Will and Testament," a moving and non-traditional will. In it, she explained and bequeathed to others her core values: love, hope, education, racial dignity, and support for future generations.

Bethune died from a heart attack in May 1955.

In 1973, she was inducted into the National Women's Hall of Fame. The following year, a statue of Bethune was unveiled to a crowd of 18,000 in Washington, D.C., and in 1985, the U.S. Postal Service issued a stamp in Bethune's honor. Ten years later, her last home, the original headquarters of the National Council of Negro Women, was designated a National Historic Landmark. Today, it houses the National Archive for Black Women's History, also started by Bethune. It is the only archive dedicated exclusively to the collection, preservation, and history of African American women.

Bethune was also honored in 2022, when a statue representing the State of Florida was installed in the National Statuary Hall at the U.S. Capitol. It is the first statue of an African American in the Hall, and it replaced a monument of Confederate General Edmund Kirby Smith.

∾

BRING IT HOME: CONVERSATION STARTERS

Ask yourself: Can I embrace struggle as a natural step toward change?

Ask a friend: What motivates you to persevere when the struggle toward a goal feels overwhelming and endless?

THE DESERT VISIONARY:

MINERVA HAMILTON HOYT

In the early 1900s, Minerva Hamilton Hoyt became a champion of desert ecosystems and the driving force behind the creation of three national landmarks in Southern California, two of which later became national parks.

Born in 1866 on a Mississippi plantation, her upbringing was filled with finishing schools and social events. But her marriage in 1891 took her to New York and then to Pasadena in the late 1890s. When her infant son died, followed by her husband, she was consumed by grief. She found comfort in riding out to the desert to sleep under the stars and listen to the winds blowing through the Joshua trees. She later remarked that this landscape was one of "...strange and inexpressible beauty, of mystery and singular aloofness, which is yet so filled with peace."

As the population of Southern California began to skyrocket in the early 1900s, Hoyt became increasingly concerned for the desert's fragile ecosystem.

"Nights in the open, lying in a snug sleeping bag, I soon learned the charm of a Joshua Forest... Above, the bright desert constellations wheeled majestically toward the West, a timepiece for the wakeful."

— MINERVA HAMILTON HOYT, LETTER TO DESERT CONSERVATIONISTS

Cacti and other plants were ripped up and carted to backyard gardens for the wealthy. Large swaths of the desert were destroyed to make room for homes and highways. An avid gardener, Hoyt decided to take action. To educate others about the plants that survived in the desert's harsh landscape, she organized large conservation exhibits in major cities, including Boston, New York, and London.

In 1930, Hoyt founded the International Deserts Conservation League. A shrewd organizer, she included museum directors, university presidents, and even the head of the new national parks system as honorary board members. Soon after, she was asked to serve on a commission tasked with recommending new state parks in California. She hired and supervised teams of biologists and ecologists to gather scientific data for her report, and she worked with photographers to document the landscapes.

Hoyt's recommendation was to create parks in Death Valley, the Anza-Borrego Desert, and the Joshua tree forests of the San Bernardino Mountains. When she realized these desert areas could be better protected if they were national parks, she pursued that goal instead.

Rebuffed by the director of the National Park System, Hoyt took her case to President Franklin Roosevelt, whose New Deal included the designation of national parks. As part of a multi-pronged approach, she assembled a beautiful book of photographs of Joshua trees, some of which live to be more than one thousand years old, and had it presented to the president.

Her persistence paid off. Although not given national park status, in 1933, Death Valley and the Anza-Borrego Desert were named national monuments. Three years later, President Roosevelt established Joshua Tree as a national monument.

Hoyt didn't live long enough to see them designated as national parks. She died in 1945 at the age of seventy-nine. Anza-Borrego became a national landmark in 1974, and both Joshua Tree and Death Valley were elevated to national parks in 1994. Today, a mural of Hoyt standing amid the desert landscape can be found at the Joshua Tree National Park headquarters.

BRING IT HOME: CONVERSATION STARTERS

Ask yourself: Where in nature do I find comfort?

Ask a friend: How can we contribute to preserving and caring for our national parks?

A STAND FOR WOMEN'S HEALTH:

Dr. Elizabeth Blackwell

A pioneering advocate for women's and children's health, in 1849, Elizabeth Blackwell became the first woman in the U.S. to earn an MD from an American medical school. Seeing the need for specialized medical care for women and children, Blackwell established hospitals for women and founded the first female medical schools in England and the U.S. She also advocated preventive health measures, sanitation, family planning, and sex education.

Born in 1821 to a wealthy family in England, Blackwell was privately tutored, but when the family suffered financial losses in 1832, they moved to the U.S. and settled in Ohio. Blackwell's father died six years later, leaving his family in poverty. To support themselves, Blackwell and her two sisters opened a series of private schools.

Blackwell found her calling while sitting at the bedside of a close friend who

"If society will not admit woman's free development, then society must be remodeled."

— ATTRIBUTED TO
DR. ELIZABETH BLACKWELL

was dying. Her friend remarked that she would have fared better if she had been treated by women doctors instead of men. Blackwell vowed to become a physician.

In this era, women were generally denied a higher education. Additionally, it was widely believed that they didn't have the mental capacity to meet the demands of being a physician. Blackwell applied to several medical schools but was rejected. She later reflected: "The idea of winning a doctor's degree gradually assumed the aspect of a great moral struggle, and the moral fight possessed immense attraction for me."

Finally, Blackwell was admitted to the Geneva Medical College (now Syracuse Medical School) in New York. Her acceptance, however, was a cruel joke, as the school never intended for her to join the incoming class. As a prank, the all-male faculty asked its all-male student body to vote on whether to admit her. Continuing the jest, the students voted "yes." Ultimately, Blackwell had the final laugh. She seized the opportunity and accepted.

Blackwell suffered continual harassment at the college. Initially, she was barred from classrooms and then had to sit apart from her classmates. Townspeople shunned her as a bad woman for breaking with cultural norms.

She never gave up, and in 1849—earning the top rank in her class—Blackwell became the first woman in the U.S. to graduate from medical school. The same year, she traveled to England and France for additional training but was relegated to delivering babies or working as a nurse.

Returning to New York in 1851, Blackwell was denied positions at New York City hospitals because of her gender. She opened a private practice, but struggled to find patients. She used the time to write a series of lectures that were published in 1852 as *The Laws of Life, with Special Reference to the Physical Education of Girls*. One year later, together with her sister, who had also become a doctor, and a third female physician, Blackwell opened a clinic in an impoverished area of the city. It expanded rapidly, and by 1857, it was incorporated as the New York Infirmary for Women and Children.

During the Civil War, 1861–1865, Blackwell trained nurses for the front. She also offered internships to female physicians to advance their training. Convinced of the need for women doctors, Blackwell launched a multi-year campaign to raise public and professional support for a medical school for women at the New York Infirmary. It opened in 1868.

In 1869, Blackwell returned permanently to England and became the first woman to register with the British General Medical Council. She also launched the National Health Society to educate people about the benefits of a healthy lifestyle. Her motto, "Prevention is better than cure," was ahead of its time. As she had done in the U.S., Blackwell and two female physicians founded the London School of Medicine for Women in 1874, the first college to train women as doctors in England.

After Blackwell retired, she continued to lecture and to write articles on health and medicine. She died in Hastings, England, in 1910.

❧

BRING IT HOME: CONVERSATION STARTERS:

Ask yourself: Think about a sport, hobby, or career I love. Who were the women who made it possible for me to participate in or enjoy those activities? What do we owe them?

Ask a friend: Education segregated by gender was once the norm. Do you think it's an advantage for women to learn in the company of other women or with both men and women?

CREATING SPACES:

MARY JANE COLTER

In the early twentieth century, when there were few female architects, Mary Jane Colter broke with traditional European design to create groundbreaking commercial buildings with a distinctly Southwest American flair. Using natural materials from surrounding landscapes and artifacts inspired by Indigenous cultures, Colter's unique style paid tribute to Native American, Spanish Colonial, and Arts and Crafts traditions.

Born in Pittsburgh, Pennsylvania, in 1869, Colter moved with her family to Colorado and Texas before settling in Saint Paul, Minnesota, when she was eleven. Saint Paul was home to a large minority population of Sioux. With Colter's exposure to Sioux culture, she became captivated by the geometry, design, and symbolism of Native American art.

From an early age, Colter was determined to be an artist. In 1886, she left

Minnesota to attend the California School of Design (now the San Francisco Art Institute). To help finance her studies, she apprenticed at an architectural firm. Graduating in 1891, Colter returned to Saint Paul to teach art and drafting at a local high school. But in 1901, she landed a summer job that changed her life: as interior designer for the Fred Harvey Alvarado Hotel in Albuquerque, New Mexico.

"An incomprehensible woman in pants."

— FRANK WATERS, HISTORIAN, REFERRING TO MARY JANE COLTER

New railroad lines opening across the West resulted in a boom in travel and tourism. The influx of visitors also brought an increased demand for restaurants, hotels, and other hospitality buildings. Nine years after taking that first summer job, Colter left teaching to become chief architect and interior designer for the Fred Harvey Company.

Working long hours in rugged conditions, Colter was described by historian Frank Waters as "an incomprehensible woman in pants," riding horseback, sketching ruins, and meticulously studying construction details. It was also said that "she could teach masons how to lay adobe bricks, plasterers how to mix washes, and carpenters how to fix viga joints."

Colter also had a reputation for being a perfectionist. According to Virginia Grattan, author of *Mary Colter: Builder upon the Red Earth*, "Colter was so particular about the colors she used ...that she sometimes mixed her own. For the interior of Bright Angel Lodge, she made a special shade of blue ..." insisting " ...that the painters mix the shade exactly. They dubbed it 'Mary Jane Blue.'"

Colter was equally passionate about designing spaces that fulfilled their commercial function and created a unique and satisfying experience for the user. For the La Fonda hotel in Santa Fe, New Mexico, she hired local artists from pueblos to make the furniture. Native American designs were utilized in handcrafted ornamental details, including chandeliers and lighting fixtures, and in tiles and textiles.

Colter named her rustic lodge at the bottom of the Grand Canyon "Phantom Ranch" instead of the proposed "Roosevelt Ranch" because she wanted to evoke a sense of place. At Phantom Ranch—to this day only accessible on foot, by mule, or by river raft—Colter used on-site materials, including fieldstone, river rock, and rough-hewn wood. At Bright Angel Lodge, at the top of the canyon, she built a "geological fireplace" and arranged rocks from floor to ceiling to replicate the rock strata along the trail down the canyon. Her approach became the model for subsequent National Park Service structures, whose style is known as National Park Service Rustic.

Also at the Grand Canyon, she designed Hermit's Rest to look as if it had been haphazardly built by a mountain man, and Hopi House to resemble a one thousand-year-old pueblo. These buildings, and others in the Canyon, secured her legacy. From 1905 to 1935, she built Hopi House, Hermit's Rest, Lookout Studio, Phantom Ranch, Desert View Watchtower, and Bright Angel Lodge. In 1987, four were designated National Historic Landmarks.

However, some scholars consider Colter's masterwork to be the 1923 El Navajo in Gallup, New Mexico, which fused Native American and Art Deco elements. But Colter's personal favorite was the 1930 La Posada Hotel in Winslow, Arizona, constructed in the manner of a sprawling hacienda. She designed everything—its buildings, gardens, furniture, and china—even the hotel staff uniforms. Today, it is a museum at the heart of the La Posada Historic District.

When Colter retired in 1949 at the age of seventy-nine, she had completed twenty-one landmark hotels, commercial lodges, and public spaces across the Southwest. She died in 1958.

Colter's remarkable legacy was largely forgotten until 1980, when Virginia Grattan published her biography. Other books and articles followed, and in 1987, many of Colter's buildings were listed on the National Register of Historic Places. But in 2018, Colter's achievements were undermined when architectural enthusiast Fred Shaw self-published a nine-hundred-page book entitled *False Architect: The Mary Colter Hoax*.

Shaw claims that while researching a different Fred Harvey architect, he uncovered inconsistencies in Colter's resume. He concludes that she suffered from a narcissistic personality disorder and took credit for others' work. He believes the fabrication began in the early 1950s when Colter provided information to the National Park Service for its archive. Her responses became primary source material for the books that followed.

Today, some scholars agree with Shaw; others argue that it would have been impossible for Colter to perpetuate such a hoax. Time may tell.

∾

BRING IT HOME: CONVERSATION STARTERS

Ask yourself: Have I observed women who had to know more and do more than their male peers to be respected in their careers?

Ask a friend: What's the best course of action to take when gender matters more than skill, wisdom, or creativity?

UNSTOPPABLE COURAGE:

ANGELINA GRIMKÉ WELD

In the deep South during the early 1800s, Angelina Grimké Weld was a pioneering abolitionist who defied laws and social norms to teach enslaved people how to read and write. She risked her own life and reputation by publishing essays on the horrors of slavery and speaking out about her commitment to abolition.

Born in 1805, Weld was the fourteenth child of a wealthy plantation owner in South Carolina. Her father believed that women should be subservient to men and educated only his sons. However, his sons often shared their lessons with their sisters, who in turn taught many enslaved people on the plantation to read and write.

Witnessing the horrific treatment of African Americans, Weld came to believe that slavery was contrary to all moral and religious teachings. She tried to convince her parents, but to no avail. She converted from the Episcopalian faith to Quakerism, which actively supported abolition and, in 1829, she left home to join

"I recognize no rights but human rights..."

— ANGELINA GRIMKÉ WELD, LETTER TO CATHERINE BEECHER, 1837

her sister, who had moved to Philadelphia. The two became members of the Female Anti-Slavery Society.

Weld supported herself by teaching and began speaking out against slavery. In 1835, she wrote to William Lloyd Garrison, publisher of the renowned abolitionist newspaper, *The Liberator*. He published her letter, which opened the door to her career writing essays about the mistreatment of enslaved people.

One essay, "An Appeal to Christian Women of the South," urged women to join the abolitionist cause. It met with such hostility that in South Carolina, Weld was warned that she would be imprisoned if she ever returned home.

Instead, she traveled throughout New England giving speeches in support of abolition. At times, stone-throwing mobs encircled the meeting halls where she spoke. Initially, many Northerners doubted her stories. Additionally, a woman addressing an audience of men and women violated accepted norms and contributed to their suspicions that her stories were untrue. However, Weld became the first woman to speak before the Massachusetts State Legislature when she delivered a petition to abolish slavery. It was signed by more than twenty thousand women.

Like other abolitionists and suffragists, Weld believed in the Declaration of Independence and in fulfilling its promises. After one of her brothers was widowed, he lived openly with one of his female slaves, and they had children together. When the brother died, Weld raised these children as her own. One of them, Henry Grimké, became the second African American man to graduate from Harvard Law School. He married a white woman and had a daughter whom they named Angelina in honor of his aunt.

Weld died in 1879, the year before her niece was born, but little Angelina inherited her great aunt's spirit and tenacity.

Throughout her life, the younger Angelina faced racial prejudice and discrimination because of her gender and sexual orientation. She was a lesbian. But like her courageous great-aunt, the younger Angelina also picked up a pen and wrote about the injustices facing African Americans. She published short stories, poetry, and plays, and became the first Black female playwright to have her work staged in New York. She died in 1953.

The best-selling novel, *The Invention of Wings* by Sue Monk Kidd, is loosely based on the elder Angelina and her sister, Sarah.

∾

BRING IT HOME: CONVERSATION STARTERS

Ask yourself: How far would I go to put myself at risk for
a cause I hold dear?

Ask a friend: Tell me about a sacrifice made by one of your ancestors
and the positive impact it has had on your life.

FIGHTING FOR THE OTHER HALF:

Maria Guadalupe Evangelina de Lopez

Information about Maria Guadalupe Evangelina de Lopez is sparse, but what is known is that in the early twentieth century, she was a pioneering Latinx suffragist, educator, and activist for the preservation of Mexican American heritage and a proponent of bilingual education.

Born in Los Angeles in 1881, Lopez graduated from Pasadena High School in 1897 and then earned a degree in education at what later became the University of California, Los Angeles (UCLA). After graduation, she taught English as a second language to high school students, while also working to translate important historical and cultural documents. In 1902, Lopez joined the faculty at UCLA, becoming the youngest instructor on staff and possibly the first Latinx.

A suffragist, Lopez became active in the Votes for Women Club and, in 1911, she served as president of UCLA's Equal Suffrage League. She played a critical role in winning the vote for California women by focusing her efforts on Latinx women. She traveled throughout the state, distributing suffrage materials she had translated into Spanish. A powerful orator, Lopez delivered her speeches in Spanish, which was unprecedented at the time.

In her speeches, Lopez argued that California could not call itself a democracy while disenfranchising half its citizens or ignoring its Latinx population. She also published editorials in newspapers, including the *Los Angeles Herald*. In October 1911, California became the sixth state in the nation to enfranchise women. In 1913, leading suffragists selected Lopez to represent California in the Women's March on Washington, D.C.

"...[Only] half of the... inhabitants of our State of California enjoy the one great privilege cherished by the hearts of an enlightened people... to participate in the performance of a duty which is the true essence of that spirit for which our forefathers fought and bled —the spirit of American democracy...."

— MARIA GUADALUPE EVANGELINA DE LOPEZ, SUFFRAGE SPEECH

Lopez was also passionate about labor initiatives and translated voting information and other vital documents into Spanish. When America entered World War I in 1917, she moved to New York City to study auto mechanics and aviation, and then shipped out to France to work as an ambulance driver. During a prolonged attack on the hospital where she was stationed, Lopez and three other women risked their lives to transport wounded soldiers to safety. In 1918, Lopez and the other women were honored for their bravery by the French government.

After the war, Lopez returned to Southern California, married, and resumed teaching. She renewed her efforts to educate the public about California's rich cultural heritage and to promote the importance of learning the Spanish language.

Lopez co-founded the Woman's City Club of Los Angeles and was active in the Woman's College and Business Clubs. She served on the Executive Board of the

High School Teachers' Association and, in 1937, she became the president of the UCLA Faculty Women's Club.

Lopez died in 1977 in Orange, California. She was ninety-six.

⁊⤾

BRING IT HOME: CONVERSATION STARTERS

Ask yourself: How much do I know about and celebrate cultures other than my own?

Ask a friend: Does democracy exist if only one view prevails?

THE DISARMED HEART:

Lucia True Ames Mead

In the late nineteenth and early twentieth centuries, Lucia True Ames Mead was a well-known suffragist, global peace activist, and education reformer. A renowned public speaker, she championed these issues in essays for newspapers and journals and published seven books, including one novel. Although overshadowed by her more famous family and friends, Mead was a force who mentored others in achieving greatness.

Born in Boscawen, New Hampshire, in 1856, Mead was the third of four siblings. The family traced its roots to the earliest British colonists, and Mead grew up in an ethos of duty to God, country, and one's fellow man. Her ancestors had fought in the Revolutionary War, and her father served as a colonel in the Union Army during the Civil War. Her family believed in education and freedom for all.

At the age of fourteen, Mead moved to Boston to receive a more formal education. A dedicated and rigorous scholar, she pursued studies in literature, history, theology, and philosophy. A talented musician, she paid for her education by giving piano lessons.

As a young woman, she studied at the Concord Summer School of Philosophy with one of the country's leading transcendentalist philosophers, William Torrey Harris. This helped her clarify her belief in the family of humanity, rejecting arbitrary divisions of race, religion, or nationality. When Harris was unavailable, Mead led discussion groups on his behalf, and she also developed and taught courses for women. As an adult, Mead traveled to Europe with scholars from Harvard and MIT to study educational methods—part of her work as an education reformer in the U.S.

It is unknown exactly when Mead became a suffragist or peace activist, but from an early age, she adopted the conviction that women were key to cultural, educational, and economic change. In 1878, at the age of twenty-two, she was denied membership in a local church because her beliefs in equality for women and people of color were considered too progressive.

By 1880, Mead's parents had both died. She and her three siblings shared a brownstone in Boston with her two nieces and her nephew. Although of modest means, the family was at the epicenter of social change. One of Mead's sisters was among the earliest female graduates of MIT, and the other, a widow with three children, reinvented herself by taking wealthy young women on their grand tours of Europe. Thought leaders regularly dined at their table, including Lucy Stone, founder of the American Woman Suffrage Association. Later, Mead served as president of the Massachusetts Woman Suffrage Association from 1903–1909, and she remained active in the cause until the passage of the Nineteenth Amendment in 1920.

Mead published her first book, a novel, in 1889. *Memoirs of a Millionaire* is the story of a woman who unexpectedly inherits a fortune and must decide how best to use it. A thinly veiled account of Mead's philosophy, the book chastises others who fail to use their money for the benefit of others. Mead wrote six additional books, possibly more, all nonfiction, which argued for social justice and pacifism.

Mead was also at the forefront of the world peace movement. In 1897, she delivered a rousing speech on pacifism to a high-profile gathering of business,

> *"We are not, first of all, Americans; we are, first of all, human beings; we are, first of all, God's children, and we have identical interests with all God's children all over the face of the earth."*
>
> — LUCIA TRUE AMES MEAD, SPEECH, 1897

academic, and community leaders. Although it was rare for women to address an audience of mostly men, the speech catapulted her into the international spotlight. Later, amid the rising tide of nationalism pre-World War I, she stood firm in her pacifist views despite sharp criticism that she was "unpatriotic." In 1915, she co-founded the Women's Peace Party, served as national secretary, and was a delegate to several international pacifist organizations.

Like many early feminists, Mead initially eschewed marriage so as not to give up her independence. She changed her mind in 1898 and married Edwin Doake Mead, a magazine publisher and global peace activist. He convinced her that together they would have a bigger impact than apart. They were married until her death.

Mead was also a tireless advocate for racial equality. In 1926, she was barred from speaking at a Georgia college because of her views. A friend of W.E.B. Du Bois, the first African American to earn his PhD from Harvard, she supported the National Association for the Advancement of Colored People, which Du Bois co-founded. She was also a mentor and friend to Emmanuel M. Brown, a young Black man who, in 1904, founded the Street Manual Training School for African Americans in the South. It remained in operation until 1971.

Lucia never had children of her own, but she was a mentor and like a second mother to her more famous niece, Mary Ware Dennett *(page 89)*. Dennett carried her aunt Lucia's legacy into the world through her battles for suffrage, reproductive rights, world peace, and equality.

Mead died in 1936 from injuries sustained in an accidental fall from a subway platform. She was eighty years old.

BRING IT HOME: CONVERSATION STARTERS

Ask yourself: Do the politicians I support choose pacifism or militarism?

Ask a friend: What would our lives look like if we adopted pacifist principles and behaviors?

DR. GLADYS WEST

REVEREND DR. PAULI MURRAY

EUNICE NEWTON FOOTE

The Paradigm Shifters

VICTORIA WOODHULL

DR. CHIEN-SHIUNG WU

DR. ROSALIND FRANKLIN

PATHFINDER:

Dr. Gladys West

The next time you use a map or location service on your phone, laptop, or other electronic device, thank Dr. Gladys West, an African American mathematician. Defying poverty, sexism, and Jim Crow segregation, her work was critical to the invention of the Global Positioning System, commonly known as GPS.

Born Gladys Mae Brown in 1930, West grew up in rural Virginia, working alongside her parents and siblings on their small family farm. Determined to escape a predictable future as a farmer or a tobacco worker, West believed that education was her ticket "off the farm."

In high school, no single subject captivated her imagination, so she decided to become proficient in each of them. She graduated valedictorian and won a full scholarship to Virginia State College (now Virginia State University). In 1952, she earned a degree in mathematics, and in 1955, she received the first of her two master's degrees.

In an era that West later referred to as "separate but unequal," she was denied several career opportunities because of race and gender. After a brief period as a teacher, in 1956, West became the fourth Black person hired at a Naval weapons facility in Virginia. There she met and married her husband, also a scientist.

"Study hard."

— DR. GLADYS WEST,
XYHT MAGAZINE, 2019

In the 1950s and early 1960s, most complex mathematical equations were calculated by hand. West soon earned a reputation for her precision and speed in solving equations. When the Navy installed one of the first supercomputers at the lab where she worked, West often had the job of checking its accuracy. Eventually, she learned to program the computer to solve complex mathematical problems.

West was at the forefront of other new technologies, including the use of satellites to determine the relationship between objects in space. Her success in calculating the movements of Pluto in relation to Neptune led to leadership roles in other groundbreaking initiatives.

In 1978, West led the Navy's Seasat team, an experimental program that used satellites to survey and gather data on ocean conditions in real time. The satellite had to be programmed to collect data, then factor in multiple changing variables such as wave height, water temperature, currents, winds, and other elements.

It brought scientists one step closer to determining the exact shape of an ever-shifting Earth. According to West, "The Earth is not round, and we had to figure out the shape, precisely."

The challenge was to create a model that accurately measured and interpreted the Earth's geometric shape, orientation in space, and gravity field. Her success was one of the critical components that enabled the precise location of points on the planet, or GPS.

West later said that she and her colleagues weren't thinking about the far-ranging implications of their work. "The most important thing," she said, "was to do the work at hand, and to make sure it was correct."

Like that of other "hidden figures" such as NASA's mathematicians Katherine Johnson, Dorothy Vaughan, and Mary Jackson, West's groundbreaking work went mostly unrecognized. That changed in 2018 when she published a memoir, *It*

Began with a Dream. She dedicated the book to her mother and to the many "strong women in my life who said I could do it."

Like those who mentored her, West also sought to be a role model. She regularly gave speeches and talks to young women and also served as a mentor to aspiring scientists, especially those she said had "two strikes against them"—being Black and female.

It was also in 2018 that West was inducted into the Air Force Space and Missile Pioneers Hall of Fame and recognized by the Virginia General Assembly for her work in the development of GPS.

Throughout her life, West's curiosity and passion for education increased. In 1973, while working full-time, raising children, and serving on the local school board, she earned her second master's degree. Following retirement in 1998, West suffered a stroke but went on to earn her PhD from Virginia Polytechnic Institute at the age of seventy.

West remained active in her church and in supporting young people interested in science until her death. She passed away in January 2026, at the age of ninety-five. Her advice? "Concentrate on your core subjects, take a look around at all of the options, and choose what you might be interested in—and of course, study hard."

❧

BRING IT HOME: CONVERSATION STARTERS

Ask yourself: The formidable accomplishments of multitudes of women have gone unrecognized. How can I celebrate the women I admire?

Ask a friend: Are you a lifelong learner? What motivates you?

FAITH IN ACTION:

REVEREND DR. PAULI MURRAY

Note: Throughout her life (1910–1985), Murray struggled with gender identity. Today, she would likely identify as nonbinary, but in the twentieth century, gender-neutral pronouns were not widely used. I am using she/her because that is how she wrote about herself.

Reverend Dr. Pauli Murray was one of the most significant yet least well-known legal scholars of the twentieth century, whose legal arguments helped reshape legislation at the Supreme Court level and overturn racist doctrines, including the notion of "separate but equal." Murray challenged and broke gender, racial, religious, and sexual barriers. The first Black woman to earn a doctor of the science of law degree from Yale University, she was also a cofounder of the National Organization for Women, a poet and author, and the first Black woman ordained as an Episcopal priest.

She was born Anna Pauline Murray in 1910 in Maryland. Both parents were bi-racial. Her mother died four years later, and her father was institutionalized for physical and mental health issues. Murray was taken in by an aunt and moved to Durham, North Carolina.

Graduating from high school in 1926 at age fifteen, she declared that she did not want to perpetuate Jim Crow segregation and refused to apply to Black colleges. Instead, she applied to the mostly white, all-male Columbia University. She was denied admission due to her gender. Instead, she attended the racially integrated Hunter College for women. Murray graduated in 1933 with a bachelor's degree in English literature.

During the Great Depression (1929–1941), finding steady work was difficult, so Murray and a friend opted to travel. They disguised themselves as boys and jumped aboard freight cars, riding the rails alongside hobos. Murray fell in love with her friend, but her feelings were not reciprocated. Photos from this period show Murray adopting personas she referred to as "The Dude," "The Vagabond," and "The Crusader."

In private journals and correspondence, Murray sometimes identified as male and other times as female. Publicly, she identified as female, and the world related to Murray as a woman. Struggling with her gender, she attempted to have gender-affirming treatments, including hormone therapy, but was denied. She also wanted to have exploratory surgery to determine if she had undescended testicles, but she was refused. Murray later changed her name from Anna Pauline to Pauli.

Murray's instinct to challenge accepted norms motivated her to apply to graduate school at the all-white University of North Carolina (UNC) in 1938. In her application, she argued that two of her white ancestors had attended the college and that one relative was then serving on its board of directors. UNC denied Murray's admission on the basis of race. In response, she launched a letter-writing campaign to call attention to the educational disparities facing African Americans.

In a letter to President Franklin D. Roosevelt, Murray accused him of caring more about fascism abroad than racism at home. The president shared the letter with his wife, Eleanor, who responded to Murray, igniting a lifelong friendship.

In 1940, Murray was arrested and jailed for refusing to sit in the "Colored" section of a public bus—fourteen years before Rosa Parks sparked a national protest over

> *"True emancipation lies in the acceptance of the whole past, in deriving strength from all my roots, in facing up to the degradation as well as the dignity of my ancestors."*
>
> — PAULI MURRAY, *PROUD SHOES: THE STORY OF AN AMERICAN FAMILY*

a similar incident. Convinced she could win in court and have the law revoked, Murray planned to fight, but didn't get the chance. The judge reduced her sentence, resulting in the dismissal of the charges.

The experience compelled Murray to enroll in a master's program in law at Howard University. She graduated valedictorian in 1944 and won a prestigious fellowship that had allowed previous recipients to attend Harvard Law School. Again, she was rejected, this time on grounds of gender. Instead, she attended the University of California at Berkeley.

Murray's legal scholarship had a profound influence on civil rights in the twentieth century. In 1951, she wrote *States' Laws on Race and Color*, a booklet that Supreme Court Justice Thurgood Marshall referred to as the "Bible" for civil rights litigators. In 1954, one of Murray's former professors at Howard University argued the landmark case, *Brown v. Board of Education*, before the Supreme Court. He succeeded in overturning the doctrine of "separate but equal," using a legal strategy based on a paper Murray had written while his student.

Supreme Court Justice Ruth Bader Ginsburg also credited a legal opinion written by Murray as the basis for an argument Ginsburg used to argue that the Equal Protection Clause applied to women.

During the infamous McCarthy witch hunts in the 1950s, Murray was rejected for a position at the U.S. State Department because the people who had provided her references—including Eleanor Roosevelt and Thurgood Marshall—had been labeled by Senator McCarthy as radicals.

In addition to her scholarly writing, Murray wrote poetry and prose. In 1956, she published her autobiography, *Proud Shoes: The Story of an American Family*, which chronicles the impact of white supremacy on multiple generations of Murray's family. It was also in 1956 that she met the woman who became her lifelong, but clandestine, partner.

Murray achieved another first in the early 1960s when she earned her doctor of the science of law degree at Yale Law School, becoming the first African American woman to achieve that recognition.

Also in the early 1960s, President John F. Kennedy appointed Murray to serve on the Commission on the Status of Women. Murray grew frustrated that men dominated the participating organizations. She criticized the "...disparity between the major role which Negro women...are playing in the crucial grass-roots levels of our struggle, and the minor role of leadership they have been assigned in the national policy-making decisions."

Her observation applied in other areas of her life. Murray distanced herself from the National Organization for Women (NOW), an organization she co-founded, stating that NOW did not adequately address issues facing Black and working-class women.

In 1968, Murray joined the faculty of Brandeis University. She developed classes in undergraduate legal studies and also created the first curriculum in African American studies and women's studies.

When Murray's longtime partner died in 1973, she left teaching to fulfill what she described as a spiritual longing. Four years later, she was ordained an Episcopal Priest, the first African American woman to do so.

Murray died of cancer in July 1985.

Murray's second autobiography, *Song in a Weary Throat: An American Pilgrimage*, was published posthumously in 1987 and later re-released as *Pauli Murray: The Autobiography of a Black Activist, Feminist, Lawyer, Priest, and Poet*. Her book of poetry, *Dark Testament*, published in 1970, was reissued in 2018. A documentary about Murray's life, titled *My Name is Pauli Murray*, is available on streaming services.

෨ஒ

BRING IT HOME: CONVERSATION STARTERS

Ask yourself: What is one step I can take today to be more fully myself?

Ask a friend: What is the connection between law and religion?

MOTHER OF CLIMATE SCIENCE:

EUNICE NEWTON FOOTE

In the early 1800s, when women couldn't vote, own property, or speak at public gatherings, Eunice Newton Foote discovered the effect of greenhouse gases on Earth's atmosphere. An amateur scientist and relative of Sir Isaac Newton, Foote was also an inventor, suffragist, and landscape painter.

She was born in 1819 in Goshen, Connecticut. Her family moved soon after to western New York, a mecca for political, social, and intellectual thought leaders, including abolitionists, mystics, temperance advocates, and women's rights activists.

Foote attended the Troy Female Seminary, an innovative prep school for young women founded by feminist Emma Willard. Rather than a typical finishing school where young ladies were instructed in domestic arts and social graces, the school taught subjects usually reserved for men, such as astronomy, chemistry, geography, meteorology, and natural philosophy. Foote and her classmates were also encouraged to study science with Amos Eaton, a leading scientist who taught his students to conduct practical experiments in addition to theoretical learning.

"Science was of no country and of no sex. The sphere of woman embraces not only the beautiful and the useful, but the true."

— SCIENTIST JOSEPH HENRY, INTRODUCING A PAPER BY EUNICE NEWTON FOOTE, 1856

In 1841, Foote married an attorney who was also an amateur scientist and inventor. They had two daughters and lived in Seneca Falls, where Foote became close friends with Elizabeth Cady Stanton. In 1848, Stanton organized the Seneca Falls Convention, considered the birthplace of the women's suffrage movement in the U.S.

Foote and her husband attended the highly controversial convention and also signed its Declaration of Sentiments listing grievances against women and demanding equal rights. Foote was a member of the convention's editorial committee and one of five women who prepared the proceedings for publication.

It was also in Seneca Falls that Foote built a home laboratory and conducted experiments on the effects of sunlight on different gases. Her equipment was simple: an air pump, two glass cylinders, and four mercury-in-glass thermometers. Foote placed two thermometers in each cylinder, then pumped the air from one and compressed it in the other. When both cylinders reached the same temperature, she placed them in the sun to measure the effects.

She found that the amount of moisture in the air affected the temperature. She experimented with air, carbon dioxide (CO_2), and hydrogen, and discovered that the tube with CO_2 became hotter than the others when exposed to sunlight. Foote concluded: "An atmosphere of that gas would give to our earth a high temperature; and if, as some suppose, at one period of its history, the air had mixed with it a larger proportion than at present, an increased temperature from its action, as well as from increased weight, must have necessarily resulted." This made her the first person to warn that increased levels of CO_2 could lead to global warming.

Foote published her findings in a paper, "Circumstances Affecting the Heat of the Sun's Rays," and submitted it to the tenth annual meeting of the American Association for the Advancement of Science (AAAS). Probably because of her gender, her paper was presented by a male colleague, Joseph Henry. He introduced it by stating: "Science was of no country and of no sex. The sphere of woman embraces not only the beautiful and the useful, but the true." However, he later dismissed Foote's theory about greenhouse gas in an article published in *The New York Daily Tribune.*

Three years later, Irish scientist John Tyndall announced similar findings. When he published his results, Tyndall cited research by other scientists, but not Foote. Today, scholars debate whether Tyndall was unaware of her research or if he deemed it irrelevant. However, Tyndall remains the person credited for discovering the effects of CO_2 on the Earth's atmosphere.

Foote also researched static electricity, which she called "electrical excitation." She wanted to find which gases in the air could generate static electricity. Again, when she submitted her paper to the AAAS in 1857, Joseph Henry introduced it.

This paper, however, "On a New Source of Electrical Excitation," marked the first time an American woman's work in physics had ever been published. In the nineteenth century, American women published only sixteen physics papers, two of which were authored by Foote.

In 1860, the Footes moved to Saratoga Springs, New York, and then to Washington, D.C., where Eunice's husband became the commissioner of patents.

Like her husband, Foote was an inventor, and they often collaborated. According to an article by Rachel Brazil in *Chemistry World*, in 1842, Foote's husband filed for a patent on a cooking stove invented by his wife. Brazil also wrote that many of Foote's inventions were patented in her husband's name because, as a married woman, she wouldn't have been allowed to defend them in court.

At one point, Foote remarked that in her opinion, half the patents filed were for inventions by women. She suggested that because men controlled the money for manufacturing and sought the prestige, many men ascribed the inventions to themselves.

Eventually, Foote succeeded in receiving patents in her name. These were for devices that prevented shoes and boots from squeaking, for a strapless skate, and for a paper-making machine that reportedly saved one company $157 per day in raw materials (roughly $6,113 in 2025 dollars).

Foote died in 1888 in Lenox, Massachusetts, and is buried in Green-Wood

Cemetery. Her 1862 passport application described her as just under five feet two inches tall, with blue-gray eyes, a "rather large" mouth, oval face, sallow complexion, and dark brown hair.

Foote fell into obscurity for multiple reasons, including gender bias in the field of science. Additionally, she was regarded as an amateur at a time when American scientists were less highly respected than their European counterparts.

Slowly, Foote's legacy is being reclaimed. In the 1970s, female scholars began referencing her work in academic papers. In 1992, Elizabeth Wagner Reed included a chapter on Foote in her book, *American Women in Science Before the Civil War.* But it was retired geologist Ray Sorenson who came across a summary of Foote's research in an 1857 scientific journal. In 2011, he published an article claiming that Foote's discovery preceded Tyndall's in connecting CO_2 to climate change. Since then, a short film about her life, *Eunice*, has been produced, and in 2022, the American Geophysical Union instituted The Eunice Newton Foote Medal for Earth-Life Science.

BRING IT HOME: CONVERSATION STARTERS

Ask yourself: How can I be a better steward of the planet?

Ask a friend: Can we be accountability partners in making choices that allow us to live lightly on Earth?

"MRS. SATAN" RUNS FOR PRESIDENT:

VICTORIA WOODHULL

Nearly 150 years before Kamala Harris or Hillary Clinton, in 1872, Victoria Claflin Woodhull became the first woman to win her party's nomination as a candidate for president of the United States. Running on a platform of universal suffrage, equal rights, and equal pay, Woodhull selected the renowned civil rights activist Frederick Douglass as her running mate, making him the first African American to be a candidate for vice president.

A cofounder of the Equal Rights Party, Woodhull was also the first woman to own a brokerage firm on Wall Street. She was a newspaper and magazine publisher, suffragist, and free love activist who fought for her beliefs, regardless of the consequences.

Born into poverty in 1838 in Homer, Ohio, Woodhull received little formal education. When she was a child, her father was suspected of torching his business to collect insurance money. Her family took to the road as traveling fortune tellers and healers, selling home remedies.

In 1853, at the age of fifteen, Woodhull married and had two children. The marriage fell apart, and Woodhull took jobs as a clerk, seamstress, and actress to support herself and her children. After a time, she reunited with her younger sister, Tennessee Claflin, and together they resumed the family business and itinerant lifestyle, promoting themselves as medical mediums and spiritualists.

Declaring herself a "free lover"—that is, a believer that women and men should be able to choose and change romantic partners at will—she divorced her first husband in 1865. Free lovers also sought to destigmatize social taboos surrounding divorce for women, making it easier for them to leave abusive husbands.

Woodhull remarried in 1866 and settled in New York even as she and her sister continued their business. Rather than being regarded as social pariahs, the women were regaled by the rich and famous as colorful personalities. The young railroad titan Cornelius Vanderbilt hired them as his personal spiritualists.

Vanderbilt advised the women on financial matters and, in 1870, he funded the startup of their brokerage firm, Woodhull, Claflin & Company. Within six weeks, they amassed a fortune of nearly $700,000—about $17 million in 2024 dollars. The first women to own a brokerage, they were celebrated as "the Bewitching Brokers" and the "Queens of Finance." But they were determined to use their fortune to further the causes they believed in. They launched *Woodhull & Claflin's Weekly* to promote their political and cultural views on women's suffrage, racism, poverty, and harsh labor conditions.

As a suffragist, in 1871, Woodhull made history as the first woman to testify before the U.S. House of Representatives, arguing that the Constitution gave women the right to vote. A powerful orator, she assumed leadership roles at suffrage conventions. Still, it would be nearly fifty years before the passage of the Nineteenth Amendment.

Not one to shy away from controversy, the same year Woodhull published the first English translation of Karl Marx's *The Communist Manifesto*. In addition, she ran a scandalous story about an affair between the renowned religious leader Henry Ward Beecher and one of his female parishioners. The article led to Woodhull's arrest under the Comstock Laws on the grounds of obscenity. Dubbing Woodhull

"I ask the rights to pursue happiness by having a voice in that government to which I am accountable."

— VICTORIA WOODHULL,
SPEECH, 1871

"Mrs. Satan," the anti-vice crusader Anthony Comstock had the sisters arrested eight times in six months.

In 1872, at age thirty-four, Woodhull won the nomination of the Equal Rights Party to run for president, making her the first female candidate of a major party. The nomination pitted her against incumbent Ulysses S. Grant.

In a letter to the *New York Herald* about her candidacy, she wrote: "While others argued the equality of woman with man, I proved it by successfully engaging in business; while others sought to show that there was no valid reason why woman should be treated socially and politically as a being inferior to man, I boldly entered the arena of politics and business and exercised the rights I already possessed."

Woodhull's campaign failed to gain traction, even among suffrage leaders who came to view her as too radical. Comstock's continual harassment and arrests ensnared her in costly and lengthy legal battles and forced her to spend election night in jail. Eventually, Woodhull and her sister had to stop publishing their newspaper.

By 1877, Woodhull was on the edge of financial ruin. Divorced from her second husband, she and her sister moved to England, where Woodhull became active in the British suffrage movement. There, from 1892 to 1901, she resumed her role as a publisher when she and her daughter launched *Humanitarian*, a journal aimed at promoting eugenics, or selective reproduction.

In its early stages, eugenics was a popular idea as a way of improving humanity's lot by eliminating disease and mental and physical illness. The movement later devolved into the abhorrent notion of ridding the population of those with physical or mental disabilities, and in some cases, specific races, through forced sterilization.

Woodhull died in England in 1927. She was eighty-eight years old. Although Woodhull has been the subject of biographies and scholarly papers, there is only one monument in the U.S. honoring this groundbreaking pioneer: a clock tower at the Robbins Hunter Museum in Ohio, near her birthplace.

∾

BRING IT HOME: CONVERSATION STARTERS

Ask yourself: Would I be willing to be arrested for my beliefs?

Ask a friend: What do you consider a social taboo?

ATOMIC:

DR. CHIEN-SHIUNG WU

In 1936, Chien-Shiung Wu left her family, her home, and her country to pursue her dream of becoming a physicist. She battled gender and racial prejudice, but eventually she became highly respected as "the First Lady of Physics." Wu was also the first female faculty member at Princeton University and was recruited to work on the top-secret Manhattan Project during World War II. She won numerous awards for her groundbreaking work.

Wu was born in China in 1912, an era when it was unusual for girls to attend school. With her parents' support, she received a high school education and attended the National Central University in Nanking (now Nanjing University). She graduated in 1934 at the top of her class with a degree in physics. Following graduation, she worked in a physics lab until her mentor, Dr. Jing-Wei Gu, a female physicist, encouraged Wu to continue her education in the U.S.

With financial help from her family, in 1936 Wu boarded a ship for California and earned a spot in the graduate physics program at UC Berkeley. Four years later, she received her PhD in the emerging field of radiation and nuclear physics and was hired to work in the research lab. As a student, her adviser was Dr. Ernest Lawrence, who received the Nobel Prize in Physics in 1939 for inventing the cyclotron particle accelerator. At Berkeley, she also worked with J. Robert Oppenheimer, the mastermind of the atomic bomb, who later led the Manhattan Project.

In 1942, Wu married a fellow Chinese scientist, but the surge in anti-Asian discrimination during World War II forced the couple to move to the East Coast. Wu taught first at Smith College before becoming the first woman to join the faculty at Princeton. Within a year, she was recruited to Columbia University to join senior scientists developing the atomic bomb. Wu's research identified a process that enabled the separation of uranium metal through a gaseous infusion—a contribution critical to the success of the nuclear bomb.

"There is only one thing worse than coming home from the lab to a sink full of dirty dishes, and that is not going to the lab at all!"

— DR. CHIEN-SHIUNG WU, *SCIENCE*, 2001

After the war, Wu remained at Columbia, where her work involved proving or disproving theories of other scientists. In what became known as "Wu's Experiment," she famously disproved what had been considered a fundamental scientific principle known as the law of conservation of parity. The law stated that identical nuclear particles act alike. Wu confirmed the revolutionary discoveries of two male colleagues, Tsung-Dao Lee and Chen Ning Yang. In 1957, the two men were awarded the Nobel Prize, but Wu's contribution went unacknowledged.

Undaunted, Wu continued her groundbreaking studies and went on to receive numerous awards. These included her election to the National Academy of Sciences in 1958, winning the Comstock Prize in Physics from the National Academy of Sciences in 1964, and being named the first woman president of the American Physical Society in 1975. She was also the first person to receive the

Wolf Prize in Physics and the first woman to receive an honorary doctorate from Princeton University. In 1990, an asteroid was named for her.

Throughout her career, Wu spoke openly about the sexism and racism she had encountered while also encouraging women to pursue opportunities in science and technology. Wu retired in 1981 but continued her efforts to bring more women into the field.

Wu died from a stroke in 1997. The following year, she was inducted into the American National Women's Hall of Fame. The U.S. Postal Service issued a commemorative stamp in her honor in 2021.

∾

BRING IT HOME: CONVERSATION STARTERS

Ask yourself: If I saw a workplace colleague dealing with racism or other forms of discrimination, what could I say or do to defuse the situation?

Ask a friend: Every dream has a cost. What are you willing to sacrifice to create the life you most desire?

THE MOTHER OF ALL BLUEPRINTS:

Dr. Rosalind Franklin

Rosalind Franklin was a pioneering scientist who, in 1952, discovered and photographed the double helix, or twisted ladder, of DNA—a crucial step in understanding DNA. She died in 1958 at age thirty-seven, four years before American biologist James Watson and English physicists Francis Crick and Maurice Wilkins received the Nobel Prize for their discovery of DNA. Franklin's contribution was never acknowledged.

Born in London in 1920, at age fifteen, Franklin declared her dream of becoming a scientist, a field almost entirely comprising men. She completed her undergraduate degree in 1941 and her PhD in chemistry at the University of Cambridge in 1945. Women were denied recognition as full members of the college and were denied participating in the awarding of degrees. Even after Franklin began publishing her research in leading scientific journals, she fought for pay

"In my view, all that is necessary for faith is the belief that by doing our best we shall succeed in our aims: the improvement of mankind."

— DR. ROSALIND FRANKLIN, LETTER TO HER FATHER, 1940

on par with her male colleagues and also for opportunities for promotion.

In 1947, Franklin took a research position in Paris, where she learned X-ray diffraction techniques—a skill that would prove critical to her future discoveries. Four years later, she returned to London and took a position with King's College to create and improve the school's X-ray unit for research.

One of her male colleagues was Maurice Wilkins, a scientist working to find the structure of DNA, the molecular blueprint for life. According to one account, Franklin arrived while Wilkins was away. When he returned, Wilkins assumed that she would be his assistant, a mistake that soured their relationship from the beginning.

Instead of working with Wilkins, Franklin worked with a student, Raymond Gosling, and together they captured high-resolution images of crystallized DNA strands. Using two different fibers, she deduced their dimensions and found that DNA had a structure resembling a twisted ladder, known as a double helix.

When Franklin presented her findings at a lecture at King's College, James Watson was in the audience. He and his colleague, Francis Crick, had been working at a different lab to uncover DNA's structure.

Franklin didn't know Watson or Crick, but Wilkins did. Without Franklin's knowledge or consent, Wilkins shared her images with the two men, which confirmed their theories. In 1953, both Franklin and Wilkins published papers on their X-ray data in the same issue of *Nature,* which also included an article by Watson and Crick on DNA's structure. The same year, Franklin left Cambridge to work on the structure of the tobacco mosaic virus.

In addition to her findings about DNA, Franklin discovered that the RNA molecule is shaped in a single strand and that proteins of the tobacco mosaic virus form a spiral hollow tube with RNA wrapped around it. This confirmed another hypothesis of James Watson's and became an important step in later research on the polio virus.

Franklin's career was cut short in 1958 when she died from ovarian cancer. She was thirty-seven. Prior to her death, she asked that the inscription on her tombstone read: "Her Research and Discoveries on Viruses Remain of Lasting Benefit to Mankind."

Four years later, in 1962, the Nobel Prize in Physiology or Medicine was awarded to James Watson, Francis Crick, and Maurice Wilkins for their discovery of the structure of DNA. Franklin's contributions were not included. Nobel prizes are awarded only to the living.

Franklin's discoveries might have remained unacknowledged had Watson not included a mean-spirited caricature of her in his 1968 memoir, *The Double Helix.* In the book, he portrayed Franklin as ill-tempered, incompetent, and arrogant, and as a woman who refused to collaborate with colleagues.

Although the book was a success, Crick, Wilkins, and Linus Pauling objected to Watson's portrayal of his former colleague. In 1975, Franklin's friend Anne Sayre published a rebuttal in the form of a biography about Franklin. Since then, Franklin's work has been highlighted in articles and documentaries, and her story is becoming more widely known.

***

BRING IT HOME: CONVERSATION STARTERS

Ask yourself: How should I handle someone who assumes I'm too young, inexperienced, or female to hold my position?

Ask a friend: How do you avoid making assumptions about a person's job or position?

ELIZABETH COCHRANE

BESSIE COLEMAN

ELLEN CRAFT

The Bold

IDA LEWIS

BELVA LOCKWOOD

FRANCES BENJAMIN JOHNSTON

BERYL MARKHAM

DR. JOYCELYN ELDERS

SYBIL LUDINGTON

EDITH WILSON

ORIGINAL MUCKRAKER:

ELIZABETH COCHRANE [AKA NELLIE BLY]

In 1885, twenty-year-old Elizabeth Cochrane read an essay in the local newspaper entitled "What Girls Are Good For." This seemingly innocuous article unexpectedly launched her into a celebrated career as an investigative journalist.

Born May 5, 1864, near Pittsburgh, Pennsylvania, Cochrane grew to become a widely respected journalist, best-selling novelist, and world traveler, all while bravely pioneering new professional paths for women. According to biographer Brooke Kroeger, Cochrane was the original muckraker and pioneered what was termed "...stunt or detective reporting," now recognized as investigative journalism. Her groundbreaking work powerfully demonstrated that women possessed the intellect and capability to undertake demanding and even perilous assignments.

Cochrane was one of fifteen children. Her father died when she was six, leaving the family in poverty. As a teen, she enrolled at what is now Indiana University of

Pennsylvania, but financial constraints forced her to withdraw after just one term. In 1880, she relocated with her mother to Pittsburgh and took on various odd jobs. Five years later, the *Pittsburgh Dispatch* published the article that became the catalyst for her career.

Incensed by the writer's assertion that women belonged outside the workforce and were primarily valuable only for childbearing and homemaking, Cochrane penned a scathing rebuttal. The paper's editor, remarkably impressed by her writing, offered her a job.

Her rebuttal, "The Girl Puzzle," passionately argued for women's need for educational and economic opportunities equal to those afforded to men. This piece established the foundation for her lifelong advocacy for women's rights and her deep compassion for the working poor. In her subsequent article, "Mad Marriages," she examined the societal effects of divorce on women and advocated for reforms to divorce laws. During that era, it was standard practice for women writers to use pseudonyms. Cochrane selected the pen name Nellie Bly after a popular song by Stephen Foster.

> *"Nothing is impossible if one applies a certain amount of energy in the right direction. If you want to do it, you can do it."*
>
> — ATTRIBUTED TO ELIZABETH COCHRANE [AKA NELLIE BLY]

Cochrane consistently worked to expose gender inequities and authored a series of articles detailing the harsh conditions faced by female factory workers. When the newspaper received numerous complaints from factory owners, Cochrane was reassigned to the society pages, tasked with writing about fashion, childrearing, and homemaking.

Cochrane, however, had different aspirations. She had resolved "...to try by every means to make my mission of benefit to my suffering sisters." It was not long before she moved to Mexico at the age of twenty-one. She spent six months reporting on the lives and cultural traditions of the Mexican people. Eventually, her stories were compiled into a book, *Six Months in Mexico*. However, when she publicly criticized the Mexican government for jailing and silencing a local journalist who spoke out against the country's dictator, Cochrane faced threats of arrest and returned home.

In 1887, she went to New York, where she skillfully persuaded Joseph Pulitzer's *New York World* staff to hire her by accepting an assignment to work undercover. Her task was to expose the horrific treatment of patients at the Women's Lunatic Asylum on Blackwell's (now Roosevelt) Island. At that time, individuals with mental illness were commonly referred to as "lunatics."

To gain admission as a patient, Cochrane first needed to be declared insane. She moved into a boarding house and deliberately deprived herself of sleep to convincingly adopt the appearance of a disturbed, wild-eyed woman. The police were summoned, and Cochrane was escorted away for examination by a police officer, a judge, and a doctor. The deception succeeded, and she was transported to the asylum.

Ten days later, the newspaper secured her release. Her subsequent articles ignited public outrage, and she later published them as a book, *Ten Days in a Mad-House*. Cochrane's reporting unveiled widespread abuse and deplorable conditions, which spurred significant reforms. This also solidified her reputation as a formidable journalist willing to jeopardize her own safety to uncover the truth.

Cochrane achieved celebrity status, leading to interviews with notorious criminals, activists, and prominent thinkers. Her undercover methods and her factual yet empathetic writing style captivated readers as she exposed the hidden realities of issues like political corruption, the mistreatment of immigrants, and even the illicit purchase and sale of babies.

By 1888, Cochrane sought a new challenge. An admirer of Jules Verne's novel *Around the World in Eighty Days*, she proposed a daring idea to her editor: she would attempt to beat the book's fictional character, Phileas Fogg, by circumnavigating the globe in fewer than eighty days. Her proposal was initially met with skepticism, but a year later, she boarded a steamship and embarked on the 24,900-mile journey. Her fame and public following rapidly expanded.

Following her travels, the *World* organized contests, inviting readers to predict her arrival times in various cities. The journey took her to England, France, Egypt, and multiple ports in Asia. Completing her global circumnavigation in just seventy-two days, she set a world record and returned to a hero's welcome. Her travels were commemorated on postcards, posters, and in the board game *Round the World with Nellie Bly.*

Back in the U.S., she shifted her focus to novel writing, publishing eleven serialized novels for the weekly *New York Family Story Paper*. She continued to write influential newspaper articles and covered major events, including the Pullman strike in Chicago.

At age thirty-one, in 1895, Cochrane married millionaire manufacturer Robert Seaman. When his health declined, she assumed control of his steel container manufacturing business. He died in 1904, and Cochrane went on to secure patents for two of her own designs: a new type of milk can and a stacking garbage bin. For a brief period, she was a prominent female industrialist, though she ultimately proved unsuited for the role. According to biographer Kroeger, "She ran her company as a model of social welfare, replete with health benefits and recreational facilities, but...was hopeless at understanding the financial aspects...and ultimately lost everything."

Returning to news reporting, she covered the 1913 Women's Suffrage Parade in Washington, D.C., for the *New York Evening Journal*. In her article, "Suffragists Are Men's Superiors," Cochrane accurately predicted that it would take another seven years (1920) before women achieved the right to vote. During World War I, she became the first woman and was among the first foreign correspondents to report from the Eastern Front. She visited the war zone between Serbia and Austria, where she was briefly mistaken for a British spy and arrested.

In early 1922, Cochrane contracted pneumonia. She died in New York City at age fifty-seven.

Since 1978, the New York Press Club has presented its annual "Nellie Bly Award" to a distinguished cub reporter. In 1998, she was inducted into the National Women's Hall of Fame, and in 2002, she was honored with a U.S. postage stamp. In 2021, the Nellie Bly Memorial Statue was unveiled on Roosevelt Island. Cochrane's life has been commemorated in Broadway musicals, an opera, films, and she has been the subject of several biographies and novels.

∽

BRING IT HOME: CONVERSATION STARTERS

Ask yourself: The word "courage" means to stand by your heart. How would I develop the courage necessary to root out the truth in uncivil situations?

Ask a friend: What would motivate you to push far beyond your comfort level to expose the truth?

SETTING HER SIGHTS ON THE SKIES:

BESSIE COLEMAN

In the early 1920s, Elizabeth "Bessie" Coleman defied gravity by simultaneously breaking racial and gender barriers to become the first woman of Native American and African American heritage to earn a pilot's license in the U.S.

Born one of thirteen children to a family of sharecroppers in a small Texas town in 1892, Coleman picked cotton alongside her siblings from a young age. She attended a one-room school whenever possible, and her natural aptitude for mathematics earned her admission to a Missionary Baptist Church school, from which she graduated in 1910. She attended the Oklahoma Colored Agricultural and Normal University (now Langston University) but was only able to complete one term due to a lack of funds for tuition.

Coleman moved to Chicago in 1915 to join her brother. She took a job as a manicurist. During World War I, he served in the Army in France. On his return, he captivated Coleman with tales of pilots and planes, as well as the greater social and political freedoms enjoyed by French women. According to Doris Rich, one of Coleman's biographers, Coleman's brother claimed that French women could fly planes. When he then declared that Black women in the U.S. "ain't never goin' to fly," Coleman resolved to prove him wrong.

She applied to numerous flight schools but faced rejection due to her race and gender. This only fueled her determination. She secured a higher-paying job as a restaurant manager and diligently studied French. When Coleman successfully applied to and was accepted into a prestigious flight school in northern France, she sought financial assistance from Black philanthropists. In November 1920, Coleman set sail for Europe.

Seven months later, Coleman made history as the first American woman to earn an international pilot's license from the Fédération Aéronautique Internationale. Airplanes of this era were notoriously unstable and dangerous. The particular model she flew lacked both a steering wheel and brakes. She maneuvered it with a large wooden stick and used her feet to control a rudder bar. To bring the plane to a halt, Coleman had to land first, then deploy and drag a heavy metal runner along the ground.

After obtaining her license, Coleman traveled to Germany, where she honed her stunt flying skills with WWI aces. Her audacious aeronautical acrobatics were captured by journalists on newsreels and shown back home, laying the groundwork for her eventual return and celebrity status in the U.S.

Returning in 1922, on Labor Day, Coleman performed the first public flight by a woman of Native and African descent. Barred from becoming a commercial pilot, she earned her living by enthralling crowds at aerial shows. She executed daring loop-the-loops and stunts that involved walking out onto the wings of her plane while in flight. She was also known to transfer control to a copilot and parachute to the ground.

Coleman relished her celebrity but was unwavering in upholding her dignity. Though initially enthusiastic about being cast in a film based on her life, she withdrew when she discovered that the movie would open with her character dressed in rags. "No Uncle Tom stuff for me!" she asserted, deeming the portrayal demeaning.

Coleman leveraged her fame to promote her message against discrimination. She steadfastly refused to perform before segregated audiences in the South. During her numerous speaking engagements at schools and churches, she

"The air is the only place free from prejudices. I knew we had no aviators, neither men nor women... I thought it my duty to risk my life to learn aviation."

— BESSIE COLEMAN

passionately encouraged Black Americans to aspire to new heights by pursuing aviation.

Her dream was to establish her own flight school, but in April 1926, that dream met a tragic end. While rehearsing for an aerial show in Jacksonville, Florida, Coleman's plane inexplicably sputtered out of control, and she plummeted two thousand feet to the ground. She and her copilot were killed. Coleman was only thirty-four.

Memorial services were held in Florida and Chicago, drawing an estimated ten thousand people. Journalist and civil rights activist Ida B. Wells delivered the eulogies. Despite the respect and attention Coleman had received, her remarkable legacy was largely forgotten for many years.

In 1992, astronaut Mae Jemison became the first African American woman in space. Jemison carried a photograph of Coleman into orbit and later wrote that she was "embarrassed and saddened that I did not learn of her until my spaceflight beckoned on the horizon."

Since then, Coleman's story has been recounted in books, articles, and films. In 1995, the U.S. Postal Service issued a commemorative stamp in her memory, and in 2023, the U.S. Mint issued a quarter in her honor. Today, numerous flight schools across the country, as well as several roads near airports, bear her name. Coleman is buried in Chicago.

❧

BRING IT HOME: CONVERSATION STARTERS

Ask yourself: What obstacles have I faced that eventually opened doors and brought fresh opportunities to me?

Ask a friend: Was there a time when you felt everything was against you but you pushed forward and, in the process, discovered inner strength you didn't think you had?

A HARROWING JOURNEY TO FREEDOM:

ELLEN CRAFT

During the height of slavery in Georgia, the enslaved Ellen Craft impersonated a wealthy white man to enable herself and her husband to escape to freedom. Arriving in Philadelphia, one thousand miles later, the couple became celebrated abolitionists, political activists, educators, and authors. Craft was only twenty-two.

Born in 1826, Craft was the daughter of an enslaved woman of mixed race, and her father was the white owner of the plantation where she lived. Craft's skin tone and physical features so closely resembled those of her white half-sisters that she was frequently mistaken for one of them. This caused considerable embarrassment to her father's wife. To prevent gossip, when Craft was eleven, the wife presented her to one of her white half-sisters as a wedding gift, thereby separating the young girl from her mother and her home. Craft was profoundly traumatized by this experience.

When Craft married an enslaved man named William, the couple understood that their children could be sold at any time, and they feared starting a family. In 1848, they devised an ingenious and dangerous escape plan.

Instead of fleeing under the cover of darkness, they resolved to travel during daylight with Ellen disguised as a wealthy white man, accompanied by her "slave," William. Ellen Craft knew she would need to sign hotel registers and, being illiterate, she pretended that an injury made it impossible for her to write. To ensure William remained at her side, she feigned illness.

"I had much rather starve in England, a free woman, than be a slave for the best man that ever breathed upon the American continent."

— ELLEN CRAFT, 1852

In preparation for the journey, the Crafts planned for multiple contingencies. A skilled seamstress, Ellen Craft carefully sewed and concealed several changes of men's attire appropriate for an esteemed social rank. She studied the gestures and social graces of white men who visited the plantation so she could accurately mimic their behavior. To cover their expenses, William Craft took on side jobs as a cabinetmaker. Both Crafts were regarded as "favorites" by the plantation owners, which enabled the couple to secure passes to leave the plantation during the Christmas holidays. This provided them with a crucial head start, initially making their absence appear authorized.

On their journey to Philadelphia, they traveled first-class on trains and aboard a steamship, and they stayed at the finest hotels. They encountered numerous close calls. When they boarded their initial train, Ellen Craft recognized the man seated next to her as a close friend of her enslaver. She was terrified that he had been sent to find them, but her panic subsided when the man merely greeted her with a comment about the weather. She feigned deafness to avoid any further conversation. In another instance, she was reprimanded by a military officer for saying "thank you" to her "slave."

When the Crafts successfully completed the 1,000-mile trip and arrived in Philadelphia on Christmas Day 1848, they were warmly welcomed by abolitionists. For the next two years, they toured throughout New England, speaking to packed audiences about their escape and the inherent evils of slavery. Ellen Craft frequently wore one of her men's costumes during these events.

Tragically, their freedom was short-lived. The Fugitive Slave Act was enacted in 1850, and bounty hunters targeted the Crafts. Although the Act criminalized those assisting runaway slaves, people rallied to help them escape to England.

They spent nineteen years abroad, during which Ellen gave birth to five children and the couple continued their crusade against slavery. Learning to read and write, Ellen published articles detailing their experiences. She joined the Women's Suffrage Organization and transformed their home into a hub of Black activism. In 1860, the couple published their memoir, *Running a Thousand Miles for Freedom*.

At the end of the Civil War in 1865, the Crafts returned to the U.S. and purchased land in Georgia. They founded the Woodville Cooperative Farm School to provide education and employment opportunities for African Americans. Eventually, the school faced financial difficulties and, with the rise of white supremacy, the Crafts relocated to South Carolina to live with one of their daughters.

Ellen Craft died in 1891. William Craft died in 1900. In addition to their memoir, several biographies have been written about this remarkably daring couple.

❧

BRING IT HOME: CONVERSATION STARTERS

Ask yourself: Do I value my freedom and express gratitude for it every day? Or do I take it for granted?

Ask a friend: How do you define freedom?

BEACON OF LIGHT:

Ida Lewis

In 1869, lighthouse keeper Ida Lewis captured the nation's imagination, earning the title "the bravest woman in America" for her audacious rescue of two soldiers whose boat capsized in Newport Harbor, Rhode Island. Until her death in 1911, Lewis saved many others and, until 2020, she was the sole woman to receive the Coast Guard's Lifesaving Medal, one of the nation's most distinguished honors.

She was born Idawalley Lewis in 1842; two years later, her father was appointed keeper of Rhode Island's Lime Rock Light Station in Newport Harbor. The family moved with him to the small, rocky island.

At the time, lighthouses fulfilled critical roles, encompassing national security and ensuring the safe passage of ferries and commercial ships. Situated near the Army's Fort Adams, the Lime Rock Lighthouse also served as a beacon for vessels transporting military personnel. In 1857, Lewis's father suffered a stroke, and her mother assumed his duties. However, with an ailing husband and younger children to care for, the responsibility proved overwhelming. Twelve-year-old Lewis stepped up to help. When her mother died in 1879, the position became hers.

The job was physically demanding, requiring ongoing repair and maintenance of the lamp, its reflectors, and its mechanisms. Daily tasks involved following a strict schedule to keep the lamp burning with oil, lighting it at sunset, and trimming the wick at midnight. At sunrise, the lamp had to be extinguished. Lewis's duties also included rescuing shipwrecked survivors. She frequently braved treacherous seas and storms, risking her own life to save others.

Although it remained an unusual occupation for women, Lewis was not the first female keeper. Established in 1789, the Lighthouse Service was the country's first Public Works Act. It later merged with the U.S. Coast Guard in 1939. There were no explicit policies prohibiting women from becoming keepers; however, most received their appointments only after the death or incapacitation of their spouse. Between 1828 and 1905, 122 women served as official lighthouse keepers.

From an early age, Lewis became skilled with boats, routinely rowing her siblings to the mainland and back each day for school. She was also a powerful swimmer. In 1858, she executed her first rescue, saving four young men whose boat capsized in the harbor. Her most renowned rescue took place in March 1869. One stormy night, Lewis's mother spotted two soldiers clinging to an overturned boat. Braving severe weather and icy water, Lewis launched her rowboat. She pulled the men into her boat and ferried them to safety.

As hundreds of newspapers across the country recounted the rescue, Lewis became a national hero. She received numerous accolades for her bravery, and her image graced the covers of national magazines, including *Harper's Weekly*. Even President Ulysses S. Grant visited Lime Rock Lighthouse specifically to meet Newport's courageous young woman.

That same year, the town designated July 4th "Ida Lewis Day" and honored her with a parade. Various memorabilia, including Ida Lewis–themed hats, ties, and photographs, were sold. A particular photo of Lewis, adorned with jewelry and wearing a fine dress while holding an oar, was widely reproduced as a postcard.

Her celebrity was further cemented in the national consciousness through the publication of illustrated sheet music featuring songs and dances composed in her honor. These included "The Ida Lewis Mazurka" and the "Rescue Polka Mazurka." In a single summer, approximately 9,000 visitors came to Newport specifically to meet her.

Although there is no evidence that Lewis actively supported women's suffrage, leaders of the movement, Susan B. Anthony and Elizabeth Cady Stanton, visited Lewis at Lime Rock. Anthony reportedly purchased a souvenir photo of Lewis to display on her desk.

Lewis evolved into a cultural icon, albeit a nuanced one. According to historian Jenifer Van Vleck, while Lewis exemplified women's capacity for courage and heroism, she was frequently portrayed in feminine attire unsuitable for rowing or conducting rescues. It would be over fifty years before women could vote, and nearly eighty years before they could formally serve in the military. Nevertheless, Lewis held the distinction of being the highest-paid keeper in the country, earning $750 per year.

Lewis's fame surged again in 1881 when she saved two soldiers who had fallen through the ice while attempting to walk across the frozen harbor. This rescue, combined with her others, earned her one of the nation's highest honors, the Gold Lifesaving Medal. Until 2020, Lewis remained the only female recipient.

Further recognition followed, including a monthly pension for her heroism from industrialist Andrew Carnegie. The exact number of rescues Lewis performed is debated, but estimates suggest as many as thirty-six people. She performed her last rescue at age sixty-three.

Lewis remained at her post until 1911, when she suffered a stroke and died. That night, the bells in Newport Harbor tolled for her.

Lime Rock Lighthouse was renamed the Ida Lewis Lighthouse in 1924, making it the only lighthouse in the country named for a keeper. Today, it is recognized on the National Register of Historic Places. In 2018, Arlington National Cemetery honored Lewis by naming a road for her, marking her as the first woman to receive such recognition. Lewis is buried at Island Cemetery in Newport, near the lighthouse she once managed.

∽

BRING IT HOME: CONVERSATION STARTERS

Ask yourself: When I think about acts of bravery, do I imagine them performed by a man or a woman?

Ask a friend: Who is the bravest woman you know?

THE SECOND WOMAN TO RUN FOR PRESIDENT:

Belva Lockwood

Suffragist, educator, and international peace activist, in 1884, attorney Belva Lockwood became the second woman nominated by a major political party to run for president of the United States. She ran again four years later. Lockwood also successfully secured the right for women to practice law before the U.S. Supreme Court.

Born in 1830 in Royalton, New York, Lockwood became a teacher at age fifteen and married four years later. When her husband unexpectedly passed away, Lockwood found herself, at twenty-two, with a young daughter to support. Convinced that higher education offered the path to a better-paying job, she made the difficult and, at the time, controversial decision to leave her child with her parents while she returned to school.

Initially, Lockwood enrolled in courses to enhance her teaching skills, but in

1854, she enrolled at Genesee College (now Syracuse University) as the sole woman in the school's science curriculum. Graduating with honors three years later, she reunited with her daughter and subsequently served as head of various women's seminaries in New York State.

In 1866, Lockwood moved to Washington, D.C., and established a private school. She remarried and gave birth to a second daughter who died before her second birthday. When Lockwood's second husband fell ill, once again, she became the family's primary provider.

By 1871, Lockwood was convinced that the route to equality lay in changing laws that discriminated against women. She applied to several law schools, but during that period, there was a belief that women were incapable of meeting the demands of a rigorous career. Lockwood received multiple rejections. Finally, nearing her fortieth birthday, she was admitted to National University Law School (now George Washington University).

"I cannot vote, but can be voted for."

— BELVA LOCKWOOD, *THE EVENING STAR*, 1884

Enduring two years of what she called the "growl" of her male classmates, she graduated in 1873 but was subsequently denied her diploma by the school's administrators. Undeterred, Lockwood petitioned then-President Ulysses S. Grant, who served as chancellor *ex officio* of the university. Lockwood was awarded her degree just one week later.

Lacking a traditional male professional network and denied access to exclusive men-only professional societies, she opened her own practice. Her clientele was comprised of multiracial, working-class people, a segment of society she passionately championed throughout her career.

In 1876, Lockwood was denied the opportunity to argue a client's case before the Supreme Court. Chief Justice Morrison R. Waite stated, "...none but men are admitted to practice before [the Court] as attorneys and counsellors." Lockwood refused to back down.

She rallied support from colleagues and initiated a lobbying effort in Congress to change the law. Three years later, what was popularly known as "the Lockwood bill" passed. It was signed into law by President Rutherford B. Hayes, and in 1880, Lockwood argued her first case before the Supreme Court.

Although she didn't win that case, in 1906 she argued a second one before the nation's highest court. Representing the Cherokee Nation, Lockwood won an unprecedented victory, and a monetary award of $5 million for the Cherokee people. Under an 1835 treaty, the tribe had sold its land to the federal government for $1 million, but the government had never paid. Lockwood successfully argued that the Cherokee Nation was owed the original sum plus interest.

As a dedicated suffragist, Lockwood participated in numerous marches and campaigns. In 1884, she accepted the nomination of the Equal Rights Party to run for president, making her the second woman, after Victoria Woodhull (*page 137*), to do so. Although many suffrage leaders publicly criticized her candidacy as a political stunt, Lockwood pressed forward, convinced that it represented a vital step in opening the political process to women.

Lockwood approached her candidacy seriously, outlining her stance on key policy issues including the economy, equality, Native American affairs, and the protection of public lands. She famously asserted that even though women were denied the right to vote for her, men could. She won more than four thousand votes and ran again in 1888.

Toward the end of her life, she reflected that one day, when a woman finally occupies the Oval Office, "It will be entirely on her own merits... No movement can place her there simply because she is a woman."

Never one to shy away from controversy, Lockwood frequently found herself the subject of newspaper gossip columns. In the early 1880s, she was accused of immodesty for riding an adult tricycle through the streets of Washington, D.C., to and from court, a practice common among her male colleagues. She was also known for responding to detractors with wit and humor.

Accused of failing to pay a client's bill, she penned a short poem in her defense:

> *Oh, cruel creditor thus to sue*
> *For money charged as overdue,*
> *And go into the court and swear*
> *To things as light as empty air;*
> *And strive to get a judgment sum*
> *Before the day of judgment come;*
> *You know I'd pay that little bill*
> *Just as you fixed it in your will...*

Throughout her career, Lockwood consistently encouraged women to pursue the legal profession, often sharing her own hardships to inspire women toward self-reliance. She was instrumental in achieving legal reform for women in areas of property law and equal pay. A fervent peace activist, Lockwood served as an international delegate at global peace conferences from 1896–1911.

Lockwood died in 1917, just three years before women won the right to vote. She was eighty-six. In 1983, she was inducted into the National Women's Hall of Fame, and in 1986, the U.S. Postal Service issued a stamp in her honor as part of its "Great Americans" series.

BRING IT HOME: CONVERSATION STARTERS

Ask yourself: How can I become more self-reliant?

Ask a friend: Do you believe only women support women's causes and campaigns?

IN FOCUS:

FRANCES BENJAMIN JOHNSTON

In the 1890s, Frances Benjamin Johnston emerged as one of the first professional and nationally recognized female photographers in the U.S. Her groundbreaking career spanned over six decades, during which she served as White House photographer to five administrations. She also developed a systematic method for documenting historic buildings and actively mentored other women in establishing successful photography businesses.

Born in Grafton, West Virginia, in 1864, Johnston's family later relocated to Washington, D.C., where her mother became a political journalist and her father an official with the Treasury Department. As a child of privilege, Johnston attended private schools and graduated in 1883 from what is now Notre Dame of Maryland University. Driven by a passion for art, she also studied at the Académie Julian in Paris and the Washington Art Students League.

However, it was a gift from a family friend that captured Johnston's imagination and altered her life's trajectory. In 1888, entrepreneur George Eastman, inventor of Eastman Kodak cameras and films, presented Johnston with her first camera. She was hooked. She began photographing family and friends while learning the art of photography and darkroom techniques from Thomas Smillie, director of photography at the Smithsonian.

Soon, Johnston was hired by the Smithsonian to photograph artifacts in Europe for the museum's collections. When she returned, she was hired by Eastman Kodak in Washington, D.C., where she further refined the technical aspects of her craft. In 1894, at the age of thirty, Johnston opened her own photography studio, becoming the only female photographer in the city.

> *"To an energetic, ambitious woman with even ordinary opportunities, success is always possible."*
>
> — FRANCES BENJAMIN JOHNSTON, *LADIES HOME JOURNAL*, 1897

Johnston's work achieved national acclaim in the 1890s and early 1900s. She frequently sold her images to the Bain News Service syndicate and often wrote the stories that accompanied her photographs. She was also commissioned by national periodicals to photograph the political, religious, business, and social luminaries of the era.

Johnston's portraits were iconic, featuring figures such as suffrage leader Susan B. Anthony, author and humorist Mark Twain, and educator Booker T. Washington.

During the administration of President Benjamin Harrison (1889–1893), Johnston became the official White House photographer. She maintained this title throughout the tenures of Presidents Cleveland, McKinley, Roosevelt, and Taft, creating intimate portraits of the presidents and their families, as well as diplomats and other world leaders.

Yet, Johnston was not afraid to challenge conventions. Defying prevailing social and gender norms, she created groundbreaking self-portraits. In one from 1896, titled "The New Woman," Johnston is depicted sitting before a fireplace with her dress hiked up to reveal her petticoat, holding a cigarette in one hand and a beer stein in the other. In another image from the same period, Johnston is dressed as a man, wearing a cap and sporting a fake mustache, while holding a bicycle.

Her avant-garde images garnered respect and influence within Bohemian circles. She also earned a reputation as a good drinking companion and a captivating storyteller.

When Johnston embarked on her career, cameras were large, unwieldy, and heavy. Nevertheless, she traveled extensively in pursuit of her art, hauling large-format cameras, tripods, film holders, and glass-plate negatives across Europe and the U.S. She photographed people in swanky venues, in coal mines in Appalachia, and in rugged natural landscapes such as Mammoth Cave.

Outspoken and passionate about progressive education, Johnston documented students at public schools in Washington, D.C., and at the newly opened Black colleges, Tuskegee Institute in Alabama and the Hampton Institute in Virginia. She also focused her lens on the Carlisle Indian School in Pennsylvania.

In the 1910s, Johnston became interested in photographing contemporary architecture, landscapes, and gardens. This evolved into another body of work that she executed in the 1920s, dedicated to documenting and preserving historic buildings in the South. Grants from the Carnegie Corporation enabled her to travel thousands of miles by car, crisscrossing the South to make a comprehensive photographic survey of architecture from the seventeenth, eighteenth, and nineteenth centuries. These photos were widely exhibited and published in several books. In the 1940s, Johnston moved to New Orleans, where she died in 1952 at the age of eighty-eight.

Throughout her life, Johnston fought to advance and promote photography as an art form that rivaled painting. She also believed that women should be paid for their work. She encouraged and supported women in becoming photographers by giving lectures and publishing articles with practical tips for success. One such piece, "What a Woman Can Do," was published in the *Ladies' Home Journal* in 1887.

Although Johnston's career was revolutionary, towards the end of her life, she had already slipped into anonymity. In 1942, a philanthropist purchased a portfolio of unsigned photographs at an antiquarian bookstore. Having no idea who had made them, he showed the images to the director of photographs at the Museum of Modern Art. The director identified Johnston as the artist and, in 1966, the Museum exhibited forty-three of the images.

More recently, in 2021, *The New York Times* published a story about Johnston in its Overlooked series, sparking renewed interest in her life and work. Today, the Library of Congress has a collection of more than twenty thousand of Johnston's photographs, plus 3,700 glass-plate and film negatives. Still, no museum has ever mounted a comprehensive retrospective of Johnston's archive.

∽

BRING IT HOME: CONVERSATION STARTERS

Ask yourself: In what areas of my life am I afraid to be bold?

Ask a friend: What's missing from your life that keeps you from feeling like you're living large?

THE GLAMOROUS BAD-ASS:

BERYL MARKHAM

In 1936, at the age of thirty-three, Beryl Markham became the first person to make a solo, nonstop flight across the Atlantic from Europe to North America. Flying against prevailing winds, the east-west route requires more stamina, time, and fuel than the opposite direction. The first woman to earn a pilot's license in Africa, she also became a critically acclaimed author and the first woman licensed to train racehorses in Kenya.

Markham was born to a wealthy family in England in 1902. Like many Brits seeking adventure and fortune, in 1906, they moved to Kenya, then a British colony. Soon, however, her mother returned to England, taking Markham's brother with her. Raised by her father, Markham earned a reputation as a wild child who burned through governesses so quickly that he decided to leave his daughter to her own devices.

Although she had only two years of formal education, Markham acquired other skills, especially from local tribes. From the Kipsigis, she learned to hunt with a spear, track animals, and survive in the harsh African bush. From her father, she learned the art of racing horses, and at the age of eighteen, she became the first woman in Kenya to be licensed to train them.

When Markham was in her teens, her father lost his fortune, fled the country, and left her behind. She married at seventeen but divorced soon after. She remarried and divorced two more times, but marriage did not stop her from having affairs with glamorous men, including members of the British royal family.

> *"This girl, who is to my knowledge very unpleasant and we might even say a high-grade bitch, can write rings around all of us who consider ourselves as writers... it really is a bloody wonderful book."*
>
> — ERNEST HEMINGWAY, LETTER TO MAXWELL PERKINS, 1942

In her late twenties, Markham became enamored with flying and took lessons from a World War I pilot. She flew rescue missions, transported the mail, and also scouted animals for big-game hunters including author Ernest Hemingway.

In the early 1930s, Charles Lindbergh and Amelia Earhart made solo flights from North America to Europe; however, the more perilous crossing from east to west had yet to be accomplished. Markham wanted the victory. In September 1936, she took off from the English coast. After twenty hours of flying, she encountered severe weather that depleted her fuel tanks and caused ice to block the lines.

In the early days of flight, planes lacked radios and radar, and Markham had to rely on her navigational skills and intuition. Making it to the coast of Nova Scotia, she made an emergency landing on the boggy soil. Bloodied by the crash but able to walk away, she was brought to safety by locals. Although the flight was an aviation triumph, it fell short of the intended New York airfield. Unlike Lindbergh, who received a ticker-tape parade down Fifth Avenue, Markham received no celebrations.

Markham moved to Hollywood and, while living in California, she wrote her critically acclaimed memoir, *West with the Night*. It garnered praise for the beauty of its prose from Ernest Hemingway. However, sales were slim, and the book eventually went out of print. When it was reissued in 1983, it became a *New York Times* bestseller.

Ten years later, a controversy erupted when one of Markham's biographers, Errol Trzebinski, alleged that it was her third husband, a Hollywood ghostwriter, who had penned her memoir. Markham's first biographer strongly disagreed.

While the controversy remains, one fact is clear: Beryl Markham boldly embraced the world on her terms and broke records in the process. She returned to Kenya and horse racing in 1952. She died in 1987 at the age of eighty-three, almost penniless. Several biographies and a novel have been written about her life, and films about her are available on streaming services.

⁓

BRING IT HOME: CONVERSATION STARTERS

Ask yourself: What do I need to believe about myself to keep going regardless of what other people say or do?

Ask a friend: Beryl Markham said, "I learned what every dreaming child needs to know, that no horizon is so far you cannot get above it or beyond it." What feels beyond your reach, and who can mentor you to reach your farthest horizon?

SPEAKING TRUTH TO POWER:

Dr. Joycelyn Elders

A champion of women's and children's health, sex education, and contraception for teens, in 1993, Dr. Joycelyn Elders broke racial barriers when she became the first African American surgeon general of the United States.

Born in 1933 to a sharecropping family in Arkansas, Elders walked a path to surgeon general that was fraught with racism and rumor. She once said, "I am who I am because I'm a Black woman."

At fifteen, Elders graduated valedictorian from Howard County Training School and was awarded a scholarship to college. With money earned from scrubbing floors and funds contributed by her brothers from picking cotton, she was able to attend. At the time, Elders' highest ambition was to be a lab technician. That changed when she heard a speech by Dr. Edith Irby Jones, the first African American woman to attend the University of Arkansas Medical

School. Elders decided that she, too, wanted to be a physician.

Elders received her undergraduate degree in three years and, in 1952, she joined the Army, where she served as a physical therapist. Three years later, she enrolled at the Arkansas School of Medical Sciences and earned her MD, specializing in pediatric endocrinology, in 1960. Elders was the only woman in her class. At the time, less than 7 percent of doctors in the U.S. were women, and less than 2 percent were African American. She did her residency at the University of Arkansas and was later named chief pediatric resident. She also earned a master's degree in biochemistry and went on to become a full professor.

> *"You can't be what you don't see."*
>
> — DR. JOYCELYN ELDERS,
> U.S. SURGEON GENERAL,
> *THE NEW YORK TIMES*, 1994

By 1987, when Governor Bill Clinton appointed her director of the Arkansas Department of Health, Elders had a reputation as an unstoppable advocate for women and teens. Her efforts resulted in the state legislature implementing a curriculum that included sex education, substance abuse prevention, and programs to build self-esteem. She also expanded the state's prenatal care and nearly doubled the number of childhood immunizations.

When Clinton became president in 1993, he nominated Elders for U.S. surgeon general. Her appointment met with strong opposition, which she believed was due to sexism and racism. Ultimately, she was approved.

Despite her many achievements, Elders' political career was marred by controversy. She was outspoken in her support of abortion and contraception for teens. She was also an advocate for AIDS patients.

Elders also generated controversy within the Black community. A Christian, she rebuked Black men and African American ministers for "exploiting Black women and stripping them of their reproductive health choices." Declaring unwanted pregnancies to be a form of slavery, she said, "If you can't control your reproduction, you can't control your life." Her views proved too much for political and religious conservatives. Eighteen months after being sworn in as surgeon general, Elders was forced to resign.

In a 1994 interview with Claudia Dreifus of *The New York Times*, Elders remarked, "Some people in the American Medical Association...didn't even know that I was a physician. They don't expect a Black female to have accomplished what I have and to have done the things that I have."

After leaving office, Dr. Elders returned to teaching. She became a professor of pediatrics and lectured widely on the importance of sex education in schools. In partnership with the University of Minnesota, in 2009, she established the nation's first chair in sexual health education. As of this writing, Elders is ninety-one and serves as professor emerita of pediatrics at the University of Arkansas for Medical Sciences.

❧

BRING IT HOME: CONVERSATION STARTERS

Ask yourself: Can I respect statistics but not be limited by them when pursuing my goals?

Ask a friend: Dr. Elders admonished religious leaders for their positions on Black women's reproductive rights. When someone expresses a harmful position, do you address it calmly, directly, and face-to-face? Why or why not?

SHE OUTRODE PAUL REVERE:

SYBIL LUDINGTON

In 1777, sixteen-year-old Sybil Ludington galloped into history, riding through the night and pouring rain, dodging British troops and marauding bandits, to warn that the British were attacking Danbury, Connecticut. She covered a distance of almost forty miles, nearly triple that of Paul Revere's more famous ride.

Born on April 5, 1761, in Kent, New York, Ludington was the oldest of twelve children. Her father had served as an officer in the British military, but when the American Revolution began, he joined the Continental Army. The family's farm was located in an area between Connecticut and Long Island Sound, making it especially vulnerable to British attack.

On April 26, two weeks after Ludington's sixteenth birthday, a messenger arrived at her home to warn her father, commander of the local militia, that the town of Danbury was under attack. In addition to being a colonial stronghold, Danbury had an important munitions depot. Ludington's father needed to assemble his forces, but having released his men to their farms for planting season, his soldiers were scattered widely about the countryside.

> *"Listen, my children, and you shall hear*
>
> *Of a lovely feminine Paul Revere*
>
> *Who rode an equally famous ride*
>
> *Through a different part of the countryside,*
>
> *Where Sybil Ludington's name recalls*
>
> *A ride as daring as that of Paul's."*
>
> — BERTON BRADLEY

The story goes that Ludington jumped on her horse and rode into the night, sounding the alarm. Some accounts claim that she volunteered, while others say that her father asked for help. In either case, she risked capture as she galloped through the dark woods in a heavy storm. Ludington covered about forty miles. She knew the countryside and where her father's men lived. By daybreak, when she arrived home, many of her father's soldiers were assembled. They were too late to defend Danbury, but they engaged the departing British and successfully drove them back to Long Island Sound.

Allegedly, Ludington's heroic efforts were widely praised, with even George Washington personally thanking the young woman.

After the war, at the age of twenty-three, Ludington married Edmund Ogden and moved to Catskill, New York. They had one child. When her husband died in 1799, Ludington worked at a tavern to fund her son's education. He became a prominent lawyer and was later elected to the New York State Assembly.

Ludington died in 1839 at the age of seventy-seven.

Although Ludington's story has captured the public's imagination, according to a 2022 article in *Smithsonian* by Abigail Tucker, some scholars doubt its authenticity. They cite the fact that there are no official accounts of her ride from the period and also discrepancies in the spelling of her name. However, Tucker also mentions that the earliest known reference to Ludington occurs in an 1854 letter by her nephew, Charles, who sought recognition for his aunt's bravery.

Ludington was next included in an 1880 book by historian Martha Lamb and then largely forgotten until 1907 when her great-nephew, Louis S. Patrick, published an account of her exploits. In 1935, the State of New York erected historic markers along the trail of her famous ride. Five years later, Berton Bradley penned a twist on the poem "Paul Revere's Ride" by Henry Wadsworth Longfellow.

In 1961, the Daughters of the American Revolution commissioned sculptor Anna Hyatt Huntington to create a bronze statue of Ludington in Carmel, New York. Ludington sits astride her horse, Star, galloping and waving a stick that she used to pound on people's doors. Ludington was also honored in 1975 on a U.S. Bicentennial stamp, and since April 1979, she has been remembered with the annual Sybil Ludington 50K Run, an ultramarathon that approximates her historic path.

∾

BRING IT HOME: CONVERSATION STARTERS

Ask yourself: For what would I be willing to risk my life?

Ask a friend: Have you ever insisted on a change that would correct the historical record?

THE DE FACTO PRESIDENT OF THE U.S.:

EDITH WILSON

According to the White House website, former First Lady Edith Wilson "functionally [ran] the Executive Branch of government" after her husband, President Woodrow Wilson, suffered a stroke in 1919.

A direct descendant of Pocahontas, the First Lady was born Edith Bolling in Virginia in 1872, the seventh of nine children. She attended Martha Washington College to study music but didn't like school. Later, she attended the Richmond Seminary for Girls.

While visiting a sister in Washington, D.C., she met and married Norman Galt in 1896. He died in 1908. Seven years later, mutual friends introduced her and then-President Wilson, who had recently lost his wife. The two were married in December 1915, shortly before he began his second term in the White House.

During World War I, the First Lady led by example. To garner support for federal

"The only decision that was mine was what was important and what was not, and the very important decision of when to present matters to my husband."

— FIRST LADY EDITH WILSON, *MY MEMOIR*, 1939

rationing efforts, she "observed gasless Sundays, meatless Mondays, and wheatless Wednesdays," according to author Betty Boyd Caroli. She also "set sheep to graze on the White House lawn rather than use manpower to mow it." She then auctioned the sheep's wool and donated the proceeds to the Red Cross.

In September 1919, President Wilson suffered a debilitating stroke. According to historian Eric Burns, the president was left "an invalid...incapable of meeting with lawmakers, governing, or performing the duties of the presidency." Burns also says that the First Lady controlled access to the president and made policy decisions on his behalf. "When something needed to be signed or written, she wrapped her hand around his and scrawled words with a pen."

This would mean that it was First Lady Edith Wilson, not her husband, who signed the Nineteenth Amendment into law, giving women the right to vote.

Limiting access to her husband was controversial, and the First Lady, together with the president's doctor and his secretary, went to great lengths to conceal his disability. One time, they allegedly propped him up in a car, then drove him around the city so he could be seen in public.

The First Lady later defended her actions. In her memoir, she wrote that she had "never made a single decision regarding the disposition of public affairs. The only decision that was mine was what was important and what was not, and the very important decision of when to present matters to my husband."

President Wilson left office in 1921 and died in 1924. Edith Wilson lived to ride in President Kennedy's inaugural parade forty years later. She died in 1961 at the age of eighty-nine.

~~~

BRING IT HOME: CONVERSATION STARTERS

Ask yourself: When have I concealed something and
how did I justify it?

Ask a friend: What would motivate you to conceal
a partner's illness from others?

EDNA LEWIS

FLORENCE PRICE

JARENA LEE

The Keepers of the Soul

SUI SIN FAR

NAOMI LONG MADGETT

HETTIE ANDERSON

GRANDMA GATEWOOD

SARAH JOSEPHA HALE

PHILLIS WHEATLEY

INSPIRED BY TRADITION:

EDNA LEWIS

T he granddaughter of formerly enslaved people, Edna Regina Lewis later became known as the Grande Dame of Southern Cooking. She inspired generations to embrace farm-to-table cooking and was among the first Black women to author a cookbook without concealing her race or gender.

Born in 1916 in rural Virginia, Lewis was one of eight children. She helped her family grow, forage, and harvest food on a small family farm, which instilled in her a love of fresh, seasonal ingredients. In a 1990 interview with Carole Sugarman of *The Washington Post*, she remarked, "My mother died when I was eighteen. Up until then, I never saw a tin can in my house."

From an early age, Lewis learned her craft by helping her mother and extended family prepare three meals a day. Using a wood-fired stove, Lewis could tell when a cake was done by simply listening to the sound it made. Too poor to purchase utensils such as measuring spoons, they used coins to determine the correct amounts for ingredients. Baking powder was measured on pennies, salt on dimes, and baking soda on nickels. Infused with joy and a sense of community centered on cooking, Lewis's early memories fueled her dream of being a chef.

At age sixteen, Lewis struck out alone to join the Great Migration, in which an estimated six million African Americans left the South. She moved first to Washington, D.C., and then to New York City. She married Steven Kingston, a retired Merchant Marine cook.

Arriving in New York, Lewis took a job in a Brooklyn laundry but was quickly dismissed because she didn't know how to iron. However, she knew how to sew. Her skill as a seamstress led to a job copying designer clothing for many celebrities, including Marilyn Monroe. For a time, Lewis found a creative outlet in making African-inspired dresses. But it didn't replace her passion for food.

> *"Southern is a hot summer day that brings on a violent thunderstorm, cooling the air and bringing up smells of the earth that tempt us to eat the soil."*
>
> — EDNA LEWIS, *THE ANNOTATED EDNA LEWIS*, 2018

Lewis enjoyed hosting dinner parties, and a seat at her table became a coveted invitation. In 1949, she teamed up with a friend, John Nicholson, to open Café Nicholson on Manhattan's East Side. As the restaurant's head chef, Lewis served up her Southern dishes, which became wildly popular with their clientele. Celebrities such as Marlon Brando, Tennessee Williams, Greta Garbo, Salvador Dalí, and Eleanor Roosevelt all enjoyed her meals.

Lewis's husband, however, grew uncomfortable with his wife's growing fame. In 1954, she resigned as chef but remained a business partner. She then began building her brand as a private caterer, taught cooking classes, and took a few jobs at restaurants along the East Coast.

In the early 1970s, when the demand for fresh, natural ingredients began to capture the public's imagination, Lewis wrote her first cookbook. Although women chefs were rare, and Black female chefs were almost nonexistent, Lewis used her name and photograph when she published *The Edna Lewis Cookbook* in 1972.

It was also in the 1970s that Lewis met Judith Jones, the renowned editor who had worked with Julia Child on her cookbooks. Teaming up with Jones, in 1976 Lewis published her second cookbook, *The Taste of Country Cooking*. Part memoir, it is filled with childhood memories and stories about Southern and African American traditions. The book includes recipes for celebrations such as Emancipation Day.

The Taste of Country Cooking launched a wave of cookbooks from both Black and white authors celebrating Southern cuisine. *The New York Times* food critic Craig Claiborne said it "...may well be the most entertaining regional cookbook in America." In 1988, Lewis published her third cookbook, *In Pursuit of Flavor*, with Mary Goodbody.

Lewis retired to Georgia in the early 1990s, where she taught cooking and mentored Scott Peacock, head chef at the Georgia governor's mansion. Together, in 2003, they wrote *The Gift of Southern Cooking: Recipes and Revelations from Two Great American Cooks*.

Lewis also co-founded the Society for the Revival and Preservation of Southern Food to share, reproduce, and rekindle traditional methods of cooking Southern food.

In her later years, Lewis received numerous awards and honors, including a listing in "Who's Who in American Cooking," an honorary PhD in culinary arts from Johnson & Wales University, and the James Beard Living Legend Award. Lewis was named Grande Dame by Les Dames d' Escoffier International in 1999. A documentary, *Fried Chicken and Sweet Potato Pie* (2006), traces her life and influence.

Lewis died from cancer in 2006, just shy of her ninetieth birthday. In 2014, the U.S. Postal Service issued a stamp in Lewis's honor, recognizing her as a celebrity chef.

∽

BRING IT HOME: CONVERSATION STARTERS

Ask yourself: How have my childhood memories of food shaped who I have become?

Ask a friend: Are family recipes handed down in your family? What's your favorite?

MUSICAL GENIUS:

FLORENCE PRICE

In 1933, classical composer Florence Price made history when she became the first Black woman to have her symphony performed by a major American orchestra. *Symphony No. 1 in E Minor* debuted at the Chicago World's Fair to a house packed with more than four thousand people. Price received multiple standing ovations and critical acclaim.

Price was born Florence Beatrice Smith in 1887 to an upper-middle-class family in Little Rock, Arkansas. Her father was a dentist, and her mother a classically trained singer and pianist who began instructing Price at an early age. At the age of four, Price gave her first piano performance. At eleven, she published her first musical composition, and at fourteen, she graduated valedictorian from high school. Two years later, she attended the prestigious New England Conservatory of Music in Boston, one of only a few schools to admit Black students. Price graduated in 1906 with degrees in both piano and organ.

Price later became head of the music department at the all-Black Clark College in Atlanta and returned to Little Rock in 1912 after she married. She and her husband had three children, two of whom survived.

During the 1910s and 1920s, Southern states saw a dramatic increase in racial violence, including lynching, and an ever-tightening grip of Jim Crow segregation. This period also marked a mass migration of African Americans to urban centers in the North and out West. Price and her family moved to Chicago in 1927. This exodus from the South ignited a cultural explosion in Chicago known as the Black Renaissance.

Like Harlem in New York, Chicago boasted a mingling of artists, musicians, writers, and dancers. This free-flowing exchange of ideas and inspiration resulted in new forms of artistic expression that influenced Price's work.

According to retired professor and music critic Barbara Wright-Pryor, Price's compositions are rooted in European classical tradition but are also strongly influenced by African melodies and by Black American forms such as gospel, blues, and jazz.

Price used her music to celebrate and share the stories and history of her ancestors. She incorporated African dances, including the Juba and the Cakewalk. The Juba traveled from West Africa to the Americas with enslaved people, involving foot stomping and the rhythmic tapping of arms and legs. The Cakewalk originated on plantations in the mid-nineteenth century as a game of musical chairs, with the last person winning sweets.

Despite the cultural flowering of Black heritage, African American composers were almost entirely excluded from classical music venues due to the predominantly white patronage and the established canon of European music. Black artists, including Price, often held day jobs and pursued music by working in churches as organists, pianists, and conductors. Others stayed within the racially accepted confines of jazz and blues clubs, or they became teachers.

Although Chicago was a creative mecca for Price, her marriage disintegrated soon after their arrival. In 1930, she filed for divorce and won on grounds of "extreme and repeated cruelty." She received custody of her two daughters.

To support her children, Price played the organ as an accompanist for silent films in movie theaters along what was called "the stroll," a stretch of State Street between Twenty-Sixth and Thirty-Ninth Streets. She earned money playing at church services, teaching piano, and writing advertising jingles. She continued to compose music and submit her work to competitions.

Price's break came in 1932 when her *Symphony No. 1* earned a top prize from the Wanamaker Music Foundation. It caught the attention of Frederick Stock, conductor of the Chicago Symphony Orchestra, who premiered the piece the following year at the World's Fair. The *Chicago Daily News* reported that the orchestra hadn't seen such an overwhelming response in more than fifty years, and described the piece as "...a work that speaks its own message with restraint and...passion...worthy of a place in the regular symphonic repertory." Price was forty-six.

In 1939, Price's arrangement of "My Soul's Been Anchored in The Lord" was performed by contralto Marian Anderson at a historic concert at the Lincoln Memorial in Washington, D.C. Price's music was also performed in concert halls in Detroit, Michigan, and Brooklyn.

Despite these successes, she struggled. In a 1943 letter to the conductor of the Boston Symphony Orchestra, Price lamented, "I have two handicaps. I am a woman and I have Negro blood in my veins."

Price remained in Chicago until her death in 1953. Although she had overcome racial and gender biases throughout her life, her work was largely forgotten. That began to change in 2009 when a couple purchased her former summer home, which had remained empty after her death. When renovations began, the buyers discovered more than thirty boxes of Price's handwritten music and notes. They contacted music experts, who took more than a decade to sort and organize Price's papers.

Two scholars, Rae Linda Brown and Barbara Garvey, pieced them together into scores that could be played and recorded. In 2020, Brown published Price's biography, *The Heart of a Woman*. In 2016, the Public Broadcasting Service (PBS) aired *The Caged Bird*, a documentary about Price's life. The title refers to a poem by Langston Hughes that Price set to music. Today, as more of Price's music is being performed, her legacy continues to grow.

Although Price received little acclaim during her life, pianist Lara Downes noted: "...hearing her story today, it can be tempting to assume...that Florence Price's career was not successful...it's a mistake to think that because she wasn't having her music played by every great American orchestra during her lifetime that she felt failure or...disappointment... She loved doing what she was doing. She never stopped, she never stopped writing music."

❦

BRING IT HOME: CONVERSATION STARTERS

Ask yourself: Have I allowed criticism to stop me from
doing something I love?

Ask a friend: What steps can we take to support
independent female musicians?

MINISTERING TO OTHERS:

JARENA LEE

In the early 1800s, Jarena Lee was the first woman authorized to preach in the African Methodist Episcopal Church and the first widely recognized female evangelist. In one year alone, she traveled more than 2,300 miles to spread the gospel. An abolitionist and suffragist, she was a powerful voice for freedom and one of the first African American women to publish an autobiography.

Born in 1783 to a poor but free Black family in New Jersey, Lee worked as a domestic servant for a white family as a child. Although she lacked a formal education, she taught herself to read and write.

Around age twenty, she moved to Philadelphia. She wrote that attending a church service one day, she "became filled with the Holy Spirit...and converted to Christianity." Later, she heard "the voice of God" telling her to preach. But in 1807, it was culturally unacceptable for women—Black or white—to speak in mixed

"If the man may preach,

because the Savior died for

him, why not the woman?

Seeing he died for her also.

Is he not a whole Savior,

instead of a half one?"

— JARENA LEE,
AUTOBIOGRAPHY, 1817

company at public gatherings, let alone preach. In church, women were barred from ministering to others, in part, because of the interpretation of the Bible passage: "Let your women keep silence in the churches: for it is not permitted unto them to speak."

Lee repeatedly asked her pastor to make an exception, but he refused. In 1811, she married, had two children, and was widowed seven years later. Over time, Lee's desire to preach grew, and she became more convinced that her true calling was to spread the gospel. She began to preach in fields, town squares, and in her home.

One day at a church service, a guest pastor struggled to deliver his sermon. When he suddenly stopped speaking, Lee rose from her seat and continued the sermon. Moved by her words, the pastor relented. Although he did not ordain her, he authorized her to preach as a minister in the African Methodist Episcopal Church. Over the next thirty years, she traveled as an evangelist from Maine to Virginia by horse, wagon, and ship, logging 2,325 miles in one year alone.

Lee's beliefs put her at odds with accepted norms, and she endured relentless scrutiny and criticism, causing her emotional pain. Her preaching went against religious norms in a male-dominated church, and as a free African American woman and an abolitionist, she worked alongside both Black and white people but still faced discrimination every day. As an early suffragist, she battled the dual challenges of being both Black and a woman.

In 1839, Lee broke yet another boundary when she wrote and published her autobiography, *The Life and Religious Experience of Jarena Lee*. It was among the first published accounts of a Black woman in America.

She died in the mid-1850s.

BRING IT HOME: CONVERSATION STARTERS

Ask yourself: What would I do if I believed God was calling me and religious leaders got in the way?

Ask a friend: Have you ever felt a power greater than yourself tugging at you to take action on behalf of humanity?

INSPIRING UNDERSTANDING:

EDITH MAUDE EATON [AKA SUI SIN FAR]

More than one hundred years before literary giants Amy Tan and Celeste Ng brought the Asian American experience to life, Sui Sin Far was a prolific author of fiction for children and adults. She was a travel writer, essayist, and among the first journalists to document the harsh realities facing Chinese immigrants in North America in the late nineteenth and early twentieth centuries.

Born in England in 1865, Sui Sin Far was christened Edith Maude Eaton. Her mother was a Chinese immigrant, and her father was British. Following her birth, the family moved and settled in Montreal, Canada.

The eldest of fourteen, Far was forced to leave school and take odd jobs to help support her family. Even as a child, she loved to write. At eighteen, Far became a typesetter for the *Montreal Star*. Within a few years, she began publishing anonymous articles for the paper about the issues facing the local Chinese community. These pieces often included stories of daily life, such as the foods people ate, what people did for entertainment, and cultural traditions.

Far also had a gift for writing short stories and poetry. Beginning when she was twenty-three and for the next several years, she published pieces in Montreal's *Dominion Illustrated* magazine. To supplement her income, she took jobs as a stenographer and as a legal secretary. In 1891, she accepted a position as a journalist for the daily paper, *Gall's News Letter*, in Kingston, Jamaica.

"Fundamentally...

people are all the same.

My mother's race is as

prejudiced as my father's.

Only when the whole

world becomes as one

family will human beings

be able to see clearly and

hear distinctly."

— SUI SIN FAR, *LEAVES FROM THE MENTAL PORTFOLIO OF AN EURASIAN*, 1909

Although Far could pass as white and lived in an era when Chinese immigration was banned in the U.S. under the Chinese Exclusion Act, she embraced her cultural identity. In 1896, she adopted the Chinese pen name Sui Sin Far, which translates as *water lily* or *narcissus* in Cantonese. After returning to the U.S. from Jamaica, she traveled throughout North America and lived in San Francisco, Los Angeles, and Seattle before moving to Boston in 1910.

During the last phase of her life, Far published several works in rapid succession, including *Leaves from the Mental Portfolio of an Eurasian* (1909), *In the Land of the Free* (1909), *The Inferior Woman* (1910), *Her Chinese Husband* (1910), and *A White Woman Who Married a Chinaman* (1910). Her themes of struggle for cultural acceptance drew on her personal observations and experiences of racism.

Far's stories for children reflect both the beauty and the conflict of growing up between two cultures. Her most famous collection of short stories, *Mrs. Spring Fragrance*, was published in 1912. As in her other works, she writes about being a Chinese immigrant in a white man's world, and she undermines stereotypes by creating a wide range of male and female characters.

Before she died in 1914 at the age of forty-nine, Far returned to Montreal, where she is buried. She never married.

Although her legacy has been largely overlooked, in the 1990s, scholars began to bring Sui Sin Far to light. Annette White-Parks authored *Sui Sin Far/Edith Maude Eaton: A Literary Biography*, and Mary Chapman wrote *Becoming Sui Sin Far: Early Fiction, Journalism, and Travel Writing*.

In a blog post for the American Writers' Museum, journalist Ben Railton said: "Far's themes of immigration and exclusion, cultural identity and mixture, and the relationship between America and China...continue to echo and evolve into our own moment, making Far's works as contemporary and crucial as any in American literary history."

⌒⌿

BRING IT HOME: CONVERSATION STARTERS

Ask yourself: What beliefs do I have that perpetuate stereotypes?

Ask a friend: Would you embrace your heritage even if it meant derision and worse?

MENTOR TO MANY:

Naomi Long Madgett

At her funeral in 2020, award-winning poet, groundbreaking publisher, and educator Naomi Long Madgett was eulogized as "the godmother of African-American poetry" for her devotion to mentoring and empowering Black writers. In a documentary about her life, *Star by Star*, she remarked that she "felt that publishing other poets was more important than the work of one poet."

Born in Norfolk, Virginia, in 1923, Madgett was the youngest of three children and grew up in New Jersey and Missouri. She began writing at an early age, and when she was thirteen, she published her first poem. At seventeen, she published her first collection of poetry. Ten years later, her work was included in an anthology of African American poets alongside that of her early mentor, Langston Hughes.

Madgett was a believer in education. She earned her bachelor's degree at Virginia State University in 1945, her Master of Education at Wayne State University in

1956, and her PhD at Greenwich University in 1980.

Madgett embodied the tenacity of the opening line of *Midway*, one of her most famous poems. It reads: "I've come this far to freedom and I won't turn back."

"Mighty mountains loom before me and I won't stop now."

— NAOMI LONG MADGETT, FROM THE POEM, *MIDWAY*, 1959

Although she experienced early success, she was frustrated by the lack of opportunities for Black writers and was unable to find a suitable publisher for her fourth book. In 1972, she launched her own imprint, Lotus Press. Even as its literary prestige grew, Madgett ran the company from her home, mostly by herself. Small but mighty, Lotus Press introduced the world to many now-famous African American writers including Gayl Jones, Haki Madhubuti, and Dudley Randall.

While nurturing the careers of others, Madgett also became a successful poet. At the time of her death, she had published eleven collections of poetry, an autobiography, and won numerous awards. She also served as Detroit's Poet Laureate from 2001–2020.

Madgett was always an educator at heart. She began teaching at Northeastern University in 1968. When she discovered that the literature departments of Detroit public high schools didn't include Black authors, she created her own curriculum, which was later adopted by the school system. She also taught college classes in creative writing.

Described as having a "blues-based lyricism," many of her works have been set to music.

Her eleven volumes of poetry include *One and the Many* (1956) and *Exits and Entrances* (1978). *Octavia and Other Poems*, published in 1988, was reissued in 2002. Her work was influenced by traditional and contemporary poets, including Emily Dickinson, John Keats, and Langston Hughes, and her themes often included civil rights. A devout Christian, her work also reflected her deep spirituality.

Madgett died in 2020 in West Bloomfield, Michigan. She was ninety-seven.

BRING IT HOME: CONVERSATION STARTERS

Ask yourself: How can I amplify underrepresented voices
in my own community or field?

Ask a friend: What is the most recent book you've read
by a Black female author or poet?

THE FACE OF LIBERTY:

Hettie Anderson

A fter escaping the violence of Jim Crow segregation in the South, in the 1890s and early twentieth century, artist's model Hettie Anderson came to embody the face, figure, and spirit of America in monumental sculptures, paintings, and U.S. currency. A muse to leading artists of the Gilded Age, Anderson portrayed the physical and spiritual representations of ideals such as Liberty, Fame, and Victory.

Yet, little is known about the iconic Anderson.

Born Harriette Eugenia Dickerson in Columbia, South Carolina, in 1873, she changed her last name to Anderson for unknown reasons. Around 1895, she and her mother moved to New York, where she worked as a seamstress and attended classes at the Art Students League.

One day, Anderson stepped in front of the easel to model, a decision that changed her life. Soon, newspapers lauded her for her "imposing" and "queenly" figure, and her features were described as "heroic." She captured the imagination of some of the most important sculptors and painters of the day, including Augustus Saint-Gaudens, Daniel Chester French, and John La Farge.

Light-skinned, Anderson and her family had been identified in the South Carolina Census as mulatto. In New York, she was described as white. No one knows what she told her friends, but some of her art colleagues were aware of her African American heritage.

By 1897, Saint-Gaudens had chosen Anderson to model for his grand monument to the Civil War General William Tecumseh Sherman. As the Greek, winged Victory, Anderson blazes a path ahead of Sherman, holding a torch in one hand and an olive branch in the other.

> *"There is nothing in*
>
> *Greek sculpture finer*
>
> *than her figure."*
>
> — THE NEW YORK JOURNAL AND
> ADVERTISER, 1899, REFERRING TO
> HETTIE ANDERSON

Describing Anderson to his niece, Saint-Gaudens wrote, "...I commence the nude of Victory from a South Carolinian girl with a figure like a goddess." He described her as "the handsomest model I have ever seen of either sex..."

Anderson again posed as Lady Liberty for Saint-Gaudens when he received the commission to design new American coins. Borrowing from the Sherman monument, Anderson's likeness appears on one side of Saint-Gaudens' $20 gold coin.

Saint-Gaudens died in 1907, but Anderson's place as one of the most sought-after muses was secure. She portrayed the goddess Athena for John La Farge in his mural for the Bowdoin College Museum of Art. She posed for Daniel Chester French's *The Spirit of Life*, a sculptural monument in Saratoga Springs, New York. Anderson's figure can also be seen on the doors of the Boston Public Library, and she appears in a mural by Edwin Blashfield at the Library of Congress. There is evidence that she posed for Adolph Alexander Weinman's sculpture *Civic Fame*, which crowns New York City's Municipal Building.

In the 1890s, Saint-Gaudens made a bronze bust of Anderson and gave it to her as a gift. Anderson copyrighted the portrait. After his death in 1907, she loaned it to a traveling retrospective of his work. However, when Saint-Gaudens' heirs requested permission to make replicas of the bust, Anderson refused. This led to a dispute with the family, who then omitted her identity and the bust from the sculptor's catalog of work. The feud contributed to Anderson's name being disassociated from the artist she had inspired.

In the 1910s, the art world underwent a radical change with the growing influence of Cubism and Modernism. By the time World War I ended in 1918, Greek-inspired monuments fell out of favor. Anderson's career faded, and she took a job at the Metropolitan Museum of Art as a classroom attendant. By this time, the museum had begun collecting works by many of the artists for whom she had modeled. It is unknown whether Anderson shared her personal connection to these works with her museum colleagues.

Anderson died in 1938 from heart failure at age sixty-four. She is buried in an unmarked grave in her family plot near her birthplace in South Carolina.

Largely unknown until the late 1990s, Willow Hagans, a cousin and independent researcher, learned Anderson's story from an elderly grandmother. Hagans and her husband began researching and publishing scholarly articles about Anderson. In August 2021, *The New York Times* featured Anderson in its "Overlooked" series, and in 2023, the City of Columbia and the South Carolina Department of Archives and History erected a plaque in her honor at the site of her birthplace.

❧

BRING IT HOME: CONVERSATION STARTERS

Ask yourself: Have I assumed all classic representations
of the female person were white?

Ask a friend: Have you ever assumed someone was a particular
race or gender only to discover you were wrong?

THE HEALING POWER OF HIKING:

EMMA ROWENA "GRANDMA" GATEWOOD

On May 3, 1955, sixty-seven-year-old Emma Rowena Gatewood told her adult children that she was going for a walk. Four months and 2,168 miles later, "Grandma" Gatewood, as she was known, became the first woman to solo hike the Appalachian Trail. She wore out six pairs of Keds sneakers. She went on to become the first person to make the trek three times. But her legacy encompasses more than meeting challenges along the trail; she also had to conquer the wounds of poverty and of physical and mental abuse.

Born Emma Rowena Caldwell in 1887 to a farming couple in southern Ohio, Gatewood was one of fifteen children. To help support the family—her father was an alcoholic and a gambler—she left school after the eighth grade to work odd jobs. A prolific reader, she was captivated by the use of plants for medicine and food. She also enjoyed reading encyclopedias and Greek classics. As an adult, she wrote poetry.

"If you will go with me
to the mountains

And sleep on the
leaf-carpeted floors

And enjoy the bigness
of nature

And the beauty of all
out-of-doors,

You'll find your
troubles fading

And feel the Creator
was not man

That made lovely
mountains and forests

Which only a Supreme
Power can."

— EMMA GATEWOOD,
"THE REWARDS OF NATURE"

In 1907, at age nineteen, Gatewood married a respected schoolteacher who was also a tobacco farmer. He became abusive, often beating Gatewood almost to death. When she fought back, he would threaten to commit her to an asylum and take away their eleven children. To escape, Gatewood would flee to the woods to find peace. But living in an era and a part of the country where women were rarely permitted the right to divorce, Gatewood had few options. In 1924, her husband was convicted of killing a man, but there was no reprieve for Gatewood: her husband's sentence was commuted because he had a farm to run and children to feed.

It took Gatewood another fifteen years to break free. In 1939, during one of her husband's violent attacks, she threw a sack of flour at him, and he called the police. She was arrested. Seeing Gatewood's broken teeth and cracked ribs, the town mayor helped her find a place to live and also a job. The next year, she successfully filed for divorce and won custody of her three minor children.

In the early 1950s, Gatewood found a discarded issue of *National Geographic* that included an article about men hiking the Appalachian Trail. Deciding that if men could do it, she could too, she made her first attempt in 1954. The hike was more difficult than she expected, and her first attempt failed. The following year, Gatewood slung a bag over her shoulder and tried again. Lacking a sleeping bag, tent, or rain gear, she slept on piles of leaves and rigged a shower curtain to keep herself dry. When she ran out of food, she foraged for edible plants, relying on her self-taught skills.

Midway through her trek, *The Roanoke Times*, a Virginia newspaper, ran a story about her journey. Other media followed suit and began reporting on her progress as she hiked. Reporters referred to her as a "jovial little grandmother," which spurred strangers to greet her along the trail with food, clothes, and places to sleep.

By the time Gatewood completed the Appalachian Trail in September 1955, she was a national celebrity. She used her platform to encourage women and girls to explore the outdoors and pursue their dreams. And yet, Gatewood never explained what her own dream was.

According to a 2015 article in *The Washington Post* by Diana Reese, she gave varying accounts of what had inspired her journey, and she led reporters to believe that she was a widow, not a victim of domestic violence. One of her daughters suggested that Gatewood's motivation was independence: "She was alone, she was free. She didn't have to answer to anyone."

After Gatewood solo hiked the trail a second time and also summited six mountains, she read about the legions of pioneer women who had walked the 2,000-mile Oregon Trail. This time, Gatewood's motivation was clear: to pay tribute to the women's courage. At age seventy-one, Gatewood followed in their footsteps, but she did it alone. Averaging twenty-two miles per day, she walked from Independence, Missouri, to Portland, Oregon, in three months.

Gatewood also used her celebrity to advocate for the creation and preservation of more state and national trails. In her early eighties, she would spend ten or more hours each day clearing thirty miles of land in Ohio to connect to the Buckeye Trail. During her last annual hike, more than 2,500 people joined her.

Before her death in 1973, Gatewood bought an open-ended bus ticket and visited all of the contiguous United States. She died at age eighty-seven, having walked more than 14,000 miles—equal to halfway around the earth.

During her life, her numerous conservation efforts and accomplishments were mostly unrecognized, but in 2012 she was inducted into the Appalachian Trail Hall of Fame. Two years later, a distant relative, Ben Montgomery, published the best-selling biography *Grandma Gatewood's Walk*. Three years later, filmmaker Peter Huston produced a documentary about her life that aired on the Public Broadcasting Service (PBS).

∾

BRING IT HOME: CONVERSATION STARTERS

Ask yourself: What changes would I need to make to
solo hike 2,000 miles?

Ask a friend: Why do you think Emma Gatewood never
spoke about the years of abuse she suffered?

THE MOTHER OF THANKSGIVING:

Sarah Josepha Hale

With the commercialization and mythology that surrounds Thanksgiving today, it may be surprising to learn that one of the advocates for this national holiday believed that breaking bread with family and friends was an opportunity to unite people divided by distance, moral issues, and politics.

In 1863, Sarah Josepha Hale, author, editor, influencer, and social reformer, was one of the reasons that Thanksgiving became a national holiday.

Born in 1788 in Newport, New Hampshire, to parents who believed in educating girls, Hale was homeschooled by her mother, then later by her brother, a graduate of Dartmouth College. At the time, no institution of higher learning admitted women, so Hale's education gave her a great advantage. She worked as a teacher until she married at age twenty-five. When she had her own children, she continued the family's tradition of educating both her daughters and her sons.

Hale's husband died in 1822, leaving her without an income. A prolific writer, she published her first collection of poems, *The Genius of Oblivion*, the following year. Two years later, she wrote *Northwood*, a novel, and published a second book of poetry, *Poems for Our Children*, in 1829. The volume included "Mary Had a Little Lamb," a nursery rhyme still recited today.

Hale's books received critical acclaim, and she accepted an invitation to help launch and edit *American Ladies' Magazine*. Around 1836 she became editor-in-chief of *Godey's Lady's Book* and remained in that position for forty years. Under her leadership, the periodical's circulation exceeded 150,000 subscribers, making it one of the most influential magazines in the country.

> *"[Thanksgiving] is a festival which will never become obsolete, for it cherishes the best affections of the heart—the social and domestic ties."*
>
> — SARAH JOSEPHA HALE, *ESSAY ON THANKSGIVING*, 1837

In 1861, the Civil War erupted, pitting families on opposite sides of the battlefield. Hale, a New Englander, had grown up celebrating Thanksgiving, but at the time, it was a regional holiday organized on different days with varying traditions. Even before the war's first shots were fired, Hale had begun advocating that Thanksgiving become a national holiday, believing it had the potential to bring families together.

Hale had written a detailed account of a Thanksgiving celebration in her 1827 novel and began publishing editorials arguing for a national holiday. She urged her readers to "put aside sectional feelings" and rally on behalf of Thanksgiving as a holiday of healing. "It is a festival which will never become obsolete...it cherishes the best affections of the heart—the social and domestic ties...calls together the dispersed members of the family circle, and brings plenty, joy and gladness to the dwellings of the poor and lowly...The moral effect of this simple festival is essentially good...a season of grateful joy."

Hale's commitment to the idea that sharing a meal could ease tensions between groups separated by politics, religion, or even distance remained constant. She lobbied state and federal officials and, by 1854, her efforts bore fruit. More than thirty states and U.S. territories were celebrating Thanksgiving.

Finally, at the height of the Civil War, Hale got her wish. When the Union Army won the battle at Gettysburg in 1863, Hale wrote to the president, knowing that he would commemorate a day of gratitude for the victory. She requested that he do so by establishing Thanksgiving "permanently, an American custom and institution." History doesn't note whether President Lincoln was swayed by Hale's persistence or if he was already contemplating the addition of the holiday. However, within a week of receiving her letter, he designated Thanksgiving a national holiday.

Yet the president did not mandate a specific date. In 1871, Hale launched a campaign to have Congress declare the last Thursday of November as Thanksgiving Day. In 1941, more than seventy years later, it became law.

Hale retired from her editorial role at *Godey's Lady's Book* in 1877 at the age of eighty-nine. Throughout her life, she advocated for the education and empowerment of women. She helped to establish Vassar College and also published emerging female writers, including Harriet Beecher Stowe, Lydia Maria Child, Lucretia Mott, Emma Willard, and Susan B. Anthony. A true daughter of the American Revolution, Hale used her influence to raise money for the construction of the Bunker Hill Monument and the preservation of Mount Vernon, the home of George Washington.

Hale died in 1879 and is buried in Philadelphia.

∾

BRING IT HOME: CONVERSATION STARTERS

Ask yourself: The Thanksgiving myth of Native people and Pilgrims breaking bread together has tarnished the holiday for some. Can I find ways to return the day to one of gratitude and praise?

Ask a friend: Thanksgiving was intended to be a time of reconciliation across divides, whether religious, political, or other. Do the roots of this holiday inspire you to approach the day differently in the future? Why or why not?

FINDING HER VOICE:

Phillis Wheatley

At about age seven, Phillis Wheatley was captured by slave traders in Gambia and in 1761, she was sold to a Boston family as a domestic servant. She later became the first African American to publish a volume of poetry in the U.S. and was also a celebrated poet in England.

The Wheatley family, whose name she took, educated her alongside their two children. Even as she continued her household duties, in less than two years, she was reading the Bible and classical literature and was proficient in Latin and Greek.

By the time she was sixteen, she had begun to publish individual poems. What brought her international fame was an elegy she wrote in response to the death of George Whitefield, a widely celebrated British clergyman who lived in London. Wheatley's poem was published first in New England and, in 1771, it was reprinted in England alongside the sermon for Whitefield's funeral.

"Her soul enlarg'd to heav'nly pleasure springs, She feeds on truth and uncreated things."

— PHILLIS WHEATLEY, 1773

With the help of the Wheatley family, Phillis tried to find a publisher for her first collection of poetry. Rebuffed by the colonists in New England because of her race and gender, she was escorted to England by the Wheatley's son in 1771. There, she was welcomed as a genius by dignitaries who included Benjamin Franklin.

In London, she found a publisher and, in 1773, her first volume of poetry, *Poems on Various Subjects, Religious and Moral*, was printed. Knowing that the public doubted she was African, the book included a foreword signed by John Hancock and other notables, as well as her portrait. Wheatley returned to Boston that same year, and soon after, the family granted her freedom.

Wheatley's poetry often included classical themes and biblical symbolism, especially when she commented on slavery. In one poem, "On Being Brought from Africa to America," she reminds readers that Africans must be embraced as God's children: "Remember, Christians, Negroes, black as Cain, / May be refin'd and join th' angelic train..."

Although she believed that slavery would be a stain on the new nation, Wheatley supported the American Revolution and applauded the country in a letter to its first president, General George Washington.

By 1778, the Wheatley family had died or left Boston. Economic times were tough for all, but especially for free Blacks, who had to compete against whites for jobs. Also, the country's resources were depleted by the war. Wheatley married a successful Black man, but within five years, the couple fell into extreme poverty. She continued to write and attempted to publish a second volume, but once again, her work was less well received in America than in England.

In 1784, she succeeded in publishing a poem, "Liberty and Peace," as a tribute to America's victory over the British. She died in childbirth later that year. Her second book of poetry was published posthumously.

Even with her remarkable achievements, Wheatley's legacy isn't without controversy. Some criticize her for not being more outspoken against slavery. Others have criticized her for allowing herself to be made an example of the idea that African people could be educated and acculturated to white standards. Yet, given the culture of the era, the criticism seems unjust. Regardless, Wheatley's poetry stands as a testament to her creativity, her talent, and her lyrical voice.

❧

BRING IT HOME: CONVERSATION STARTERS

Ask yourself: What do I do that nourishes my hunger for truth?

Ask a friend: How do you filter out the truth from the noise?

Ready to Power Up on History?

Many references are sprinkled within the profiles throughout this book. You can also learn more through the following organizations, publications, and online resources. Remember that city and state historical societies, colleges and universities, and print newspaper archives are also well worth exploring.

ORGANIZATIONS:
American Association of University Women (AAUW)
American Civil Liberties Union
American Writers Museum
Massachusetts Historical Society
National Archives
National Museum of African American History and Culture
National Museum of the American Indian
National Park Service
National Women's History Alliance
National Women's Hall of Fame
National Women's History Museum
New York Public Library
Smithsonian American Women's History Museum
Smithsonian National Museum of American History
The Library of Congress
The New York Historical: Women and the American Story
United States Mint
United States Postal Service

PUBLICATIONS & OTHER ONLINE RESOURCES:
Documentaries by Ken Burns & Florentine Films
Google Books
Google Scholar
JSTOR (subscription only, offers original and secondary sources)

Los Angeles Times
Ms. magazine
Professor Buzzkill (podcast)
Project Gutenberg
Smithsonian Magazine
The History Chicks (podcast)
The New York Times, "Overlooked" series, also "Obituaries"
The New Yorker
The Washington Post
USA Today
What'sHerName (podcast)

Do you have resources you love that aren't included here?
Send them my way. Use the Contact form at my website:

SharonSpaulding.com
WomenMakeHistory.com

Acknowledgments

To my wonderful family, friends, and readers who have nurtured and supported this collection of stories—*thank you!*

Thank you for believing in me and encouraging me, even when you didn't know I needed it. *Thank you* for inviting me to speak to your book clubs, luncheons, churches, and community groups. *Thank you* for sharing the *Women Make History* newsletter and suggesting women to feature.

Special shout-outs to:

Joey Garcia. While many readers encouraged me to publish this book, the idea for the newsletter was yours. You nudged, cajoled, and pushed me to write it, and the stories that grew from it became this book. *Thank you* for your brilliant edits, social media savvy, colorful marketing ideas, and creative flair.

Doug daSilva. You brought these stories to life with your stunning and evocative artwork for the cover and your thoughtful layout and design. Thank you for staying calm during my moments of frantic edits and overwhelm, and for always keeping me moving forward. I'm also deeply grateful for our long-standing friendship.

Miranda Spencer. Your eagle-eyed edits and corrections of my many misplaced modifiers make me look like a pro. I'm equally grateful that you're my cousin.

My writing community. You have encouraged and supported me in so many ways: Stephanie Gorton, Jennifer Jordan, Helen Frink, Trish MacEnulty, and the late David Kranes.

Margaret Chase Perry. You got me hooked on historical research and taught me how to archive.

The Wild Women of the Wasatch, the Pepperwood Vinos, the fabulous Literary Ladies, and the Radar Loves—you know who you are!

My kids: Catherine, Michael, and Jenny—and their brilliant partners, Devin, Chanel, and Brad. *Thank you* for your unending support, for saying things like, *"It's great, Mom,"* and *"You got this,"* and even for offering tech support when I needed it.

Drum roll—my husband, Carl. Your beautiful illustrations capture each woman's dignity, power, and humanity. *Thank you* for your proofreading, link-checking, and photo captions, for making dinner when I'm working, and for the countless ways you keep me focused.

Last but not least, to my parents, you'd be proud, and my always supportive sister, Sheila. Finally, to my sweet dogs, Hank, and the late Gus. Thank you for getting me up to throw a ball, or out for a nice long walk.

⁓

About the Author

PHOTO: ANITA SCHARF

Sharon Spaulding has written for *Ms.* magazine, Smithsonian.com, *New Hampshire Magazine,* and other publications. A grant from the Schlesinger Library forwarded her research on Mary Ware Dennett, a twentieth century reproductive rights activist. Sharon writes a monthly newsletter, *"Women Make History: Stories We Should Have Learned in School,"* and lives near Salt Lake City, Utah.

SharonSpaulding.com
WomenMakeHistory.com

Index

Note: The women in this book were accomplished in multiple arenas. They are organized by the issues closest to their hearts.

Photo & Image Credits

Front Cover:
  Bessie Coleman (left). Unknown photographer, *Bessie Coleman,* 1923, photograph, Wikipedia.
  https://en.wikipedia.org/wiki/File:Bessie_Coleman_in_1923.jpg.

  Elizabeth Cochrane, aka Nellie Bly (right).
  H. J. Myers, *Nellie Bly (Elizabeth Cochrane),* bust portrait, circa 1890, photograph, Prints and Photographs
  Division, Library of Congress. https://www.loc.gov/pictures/item/2017657376/.

Back Cover: Zitkála-Šá.
  Gertrude Käsebier, *Zitkála-Šá, Sioux Indian and activist,* circa 1898, photograph, National Museum of
  American History, Smithsonian Institution, ID Number PG.69.236.104.
  https://americanhistory.si.edu/collections/search?edan_q=Zitkala%20Sa.

Illustrations:
  All illustrations by Carl Spaulding, based on the following photos and images:

The Warriors:
  Page 5: Zitkála-Šá
  Gertrude Käsebier, *Zitkála-Šá, Sioux Indian and activist,* circa 1898, photograph, National Museum of
  American History, Smithsonian Institution, ID Number PG.69.236.104.
  https://americanhistory.si.edu/collections/search?edan_q=Zitkala%20Sa.

  Page 9: Dr. Mary Walker
  Unknown photographer, *Mary Edwards Walker,* circa 1860s to 1890s, photograph, *Changing the Face of
  Medicine* exhibition, National Library of Medicine.
  https://cfmedicine.nlm.nih.gov/physicians/biography_325.html.

  Page 13: Mary Ellen Pleasant
  Unknown photographer, *Mary Ellen Pleasant,* entrepreneur and abolitionist of African descent, 1901,
  photograph, Miriam Matthews Photograph Collection, UCLA Library Digital Collections.
  https://digital.library.ucla.edu/catalog/ark:/21198/z1cg1746.

  Page 17: Sue Kunitomi Embrey
  Unknown photographer, *Sue Kunitomi Embrey,* circa 1942, photograph, Manzanar National Historic Site,
  National Park Service, via https://www.flickr.com/photos/tradingcardsnpsyahoocom/7222966826/.

  Page 21: Elizabeth Gurley Flynn
  Unknown photographer, *Elizabeth Gurley Flynn,* circa 1920, photograph, courtesy of Tamiment Library/
  Robert F. Wagner Labor Archives, Roberta Bobba and Peter Martin Photographs, New York University, via
  https://www.nytimes.com/2015/02/22/nyregion/books-that-look-at-bill-de-blasios-first-year-as-mayor-
  urban-design-and-elizabeth-gurley-flynn.html.

  Page 25: Deborah Sampson
  Multimedia Marketing Group Inc., *Image of Deborah Sampson,* 2024, Generative AI, courtesy of Multimedia
  Marketing Group Inc., via https://rockfordha.org/wp-content/uploads/2024/03/3-1.png.

  Page 29: Jovita Idár
  Unknown photographer, *Jovita Idár,* circa 1905, photograph, General Photograph Collection, UTSA Libraries
  Special Collections, via https://www.nytimes.com/2020/08/07/obituaries/jovita-idar-overlooked.html.

  Page 33: Nina Allender
  Harris & Ewing, *Studio Portrait of Nina E. Allender, head and shoulders,* circa 1913 to 1915, photograph,
  Women of Protest: Photographs from the Records of the National Woman's Party, Library of Congress.
  https://www.loc.gov/item/mnwp000070.

The Game Changers:

Page 39: Elizabeth Magie
Unknown photographer, *Lizzie Magie,* 1892, photograph, in *My Betrothed, and Other Poems* (The Brodix Publishing Company, 1892), via https://archive.org/details/mybetrothedother00magi/page/n5/mode/2up.

Page 43: Eunice Hunton Carter
Unknown photographer, *Eunice Hunton Carter,* circa 1930, photograph, Wikimedia Commons. https://commons.wikimedia.org/wiki/File:Eunice_Hunton_Carter.jpg.

Page 47: Margaret Ives Abbott
Unknown photographer, *Margaret Ives Abbott,* circa 1900, photograph, The Golfball Factory. http://www.thegolfballfactory.com/the-golf-course/hole2/olympic-golf.htm.

Page 51: Dr. Susan La Flesche Picotte
Harry A. Webb, *Portrait of Dr Susan La Flesche Picotte,* circa 1900, photograph, Unknown Photographs of American Indians and Other Subjects 1840s–1960s, National Anthropological Archives, Smithsonian Institution (54752), via https://cfmedicine.nlm.nih.gov/gallery/photo_253_1.html.

Page 55: Rosalie Barrow Edge
Unknown photographer, *Mrs. Chas. Noel Edge,* 1917, photograph, The Woman Citizen (August 25, 1917), via https://commons.wikimedia.org/w/index.php?curid=122877846.

Page 59: Seraph Young
Unknown photographer, *Seraph Young,* 1902, photograph, Deseret Evening News (March 8, 1902), via https://commons.wikimedia.org/w/index.php?curid=90543523.

The Empire Builders:

Page 63: Margaret Crane
Anna Kaufman Moon, *Margaret Crane,* 1965, photograph, Frontiers. https://www.frontiersin.org/news/2022/04/20/children-in-science-margaret-m-crane-how-one-idea-impacted-women-around-the-world.

Page 67: Maggie Lena Walker
Unknown photographer, *Maggie Lena Walker,* unknown date, photograph, National Park Service, via https:// www.flickr.com/photos/nationalparkservice/35403023113/.

Page 71: Marjorie Merriweather Post
Unknown photographer, possibly Leet Brothers Studio of Washington, D.C., *Marjorie Merriweather Post,* circa 1945, photograph, via https://diplomacy.state.gov/stories/the-diplomatic-legacy-of-marjorie-merriweather-post/.

Page 75: Madam C.J. Walker
Scurlock Studio, *Studio portrait of Madam C. J. Walker,* circa 1914, photograph, Scurlock Studio Records, Series 1: Black and White Photographs, National Museum of American History, Smithsonian Institution. https://sova.si.edu/record/nmah.ac.0618.s01/ref7975?s=0&n=12&t=D&q=Madame+Walker&i=0.

Page 79: Alice Guy-Blaché
Apeda Studio New York, *Alice Guy-Blaché,* 1896, photograph, Collection Solax, via https://en.wikipedia.org/wiki/Alice_Guy-Blach%C3%A9.

Page 83: Julia DeForest Tuttle
Unknown photographer, *Julia DeForest Tuttle,* unknown date, photograph, Florida Photographic collection, via https://en.wikipedia.org/wiki/Julia_Tuttle.

The Visionaries:

Page 89: Mary Ware Dennett
Unknown photographer, *Mary Ware Dennett,* 1893, photograph, Dennett Family Archive. https://www.sharonspaulding.com/newsletter.html.

Page 95: Mary McCleod Bethune
W. L. Coursen, *Mary McCleod Bethune,* Daytona Beach, Florida, circa 1915, photograph, State Archives of Florida, Florida Memory, via https://nmaahc.si.edu/explore/stories/mary-mcleod-bethune.

Page 99: Minerva Hamilton Hoyt
Unknown photographer, *Minerva Hamilton Hoyt as a young woman,* unknown date, photograph, Joshua Tree National Park, via https://www.facebook.com/photo.php?fbid=10155318373200181&id=138794585180&set=a.10150574799050181.

Page 103: Dr. Elizabeth Blackwell
Unknown photographer, *Elizabeth Blackwell,* circa 1850, photograph, Museum of the City of New York, via https://www.thoughtco.com/elizabeth-blackwell-biography-3528555.

Page 107: Mary Jane Colter
Arthur Mathews, *Portrait of Mary Jane Colter,* 1893, painting, Arizona Historical Society Pioneer Museum, via https://hchm.org/mary-colter/.

Page 111: Angelina Grimké Weld
Unknown artist, *Angelina Emily Grimké,* unknown date, wood engraving, Prints and Photographs division, Library of Congress, digital ID cph.3a03341. https://loc.gov/pictures/resource/cph.3a03341/.

Page 115: Maria Guadalupe Evangelina de Lopez
Unknown photographer, *Maria Guadalupe Evangelina de Lopez,* 1911, photograph, National Women's History Museum, https://www.womenshistory.org/education-resources/biographies/maria-guadalupe-evangelina-de-lopez.

Page 119: Lucia True Ames Mead
Unknown photographer, *Lucia True Ames Mead,* unknown date, photograph, Dennett Family Archive. https://sharonspaulding.com/newsletter.html.

The Paradigm Shifters:
Page 125: Dr. Gladys West
Adrian Cadiz, *Dr. Gladys West,* 2018, photograph, United States Air Force, via https://commons.wikimedia.org/wiki/File:181206-F-DT527-087.jpg.

Page 129: Rev. Dr. Pauli Murray
Everett Collection, *Pauli Murray,* unknown date, photograph, licensed from Alamy.com, https://www.alamy.com/stock-photo-pauli-murray-1910-1985-was-a-friend-of-eleanor-roosevelt-and-served-32391031.html.

Page 133: Eunice Newton Foote
Note: There are no known photographs or portraits depicting Eunice Newton Foote (1819–1888). A photo of her daughter Mary Foote Henderson (often mistakenly attributed as Eunice) was used for the illustration.

Ida Hinman, *Mary Foote Henderson,* The Washington Sketchbook, 1895, photograph, Wikipedia Commons, https://commons.wikimedia.org/wiki/File:Mary_Foote_Henderson,_The_Washington_Sketch_Book.jpg.

Page 137: Victoria Woodhull
Mathew Benjamin Brady, *Victoria Claflin Woodhull,* circa 1870, photograph, Fine Arts Library, Harvard University, via Smithsonian's National Portrait Gallery, Votes for Women: A Portrait of Persistence, and https://artsandculture.google.com/asset/victoria-claflin-woodhull-mathew-b-brady/dgFMqP2o6wTueA?hl=en.

Page 141: Dr. Chien-Shiung Wu
Unknown photographer, *Dr. Chien-Shiung Wu,* unknown date, photograph, courtesy of *The Times Herald* [390 Eagleview Blvd, Exton, PA 19341], https://www.timesherald.com/2015/03/10/womens-history-month-chien-shiung-wu-was-an-influential-member-of-physics-community/.

Page 145: Dr. Rosalind Franklin
Elliott & Fry, *Rosalind Franklin,* 1946, photograph, licensed from National Portrait Gallery, London, NPG x76928 https://www.npg.org.uk/collections/search/use-this-image/?mkey=mw62979.

The Bold:
Page 151: Elizabeth Cochrane (aka Nellie Bly)
H. J. Myers, *Nellie Bly (Elizabeth Cochrane), bust portrait,* circa 1890, photograph, Prints and Photographs Division, Library of Congress. https://www.loc.gov/pictures/item/2017657376/.

Page 157: Bessie Coleman
Unknown photographer, *Bessie Coleman,* 1923, photograph, Wikipedia. https://en.wikipedia.org/wiki/File:Bessie_Coleman_in_1923.jpg.

Page 161: Ellen Craft
Unknown author, *Portrait of Ellen Craft,* unknown date, illustration, *The Liberator* newspaper (1831-1865) files, via https://commons.wikimedia.org/w/index.php?curid=25865651.

Page 165: Ida Lewis
Unknown photographer, *Ida Lewis,* circa 1869, photograph, United States Coast Guard, https://www.history.uscg.mil/Browse-by-Topic/Notable-People/All/Article/1862507/idawalley-zorada-lewis-wilson-keeper-uslhs/.

Page 169: Belva Lockwood
Mathew Benjamin Brady and Levin Corbin Handy, *Studio Photograph of Belva Ann Lockwood,* circa 1865–1880, photograph, Prints and Photographs Division, Brady-Handy Photograph Collection, Library of Congress, call number: LC-BH832-695, https://loc.gov/pictures/resource/cwpbh.04374/.

Page 173: Frances Benjamin Johnston
J.C. Strauss, *Frances Benjamin Johnston, formal bust by Strauss, facing right,* circa 1900, photograph, Prints and Photographs Division, Johnston (Frances Benjamin) Collection, Library of Congress, digital ID cph.3a47219, https://loc.gov/pictures/resource/cph.3a47219/.

Page 177: Beryl Markham
Pictorial Press, *Photo of Beryl Markham (1902-1986), Anglo-Kenyan pioneering pilot, author, racehorse trainer,* circa 1935, photograph, licensed from Alamy.com, https://www.alamy.com/beryl-markham-1902-1986-anglo-kenyan-pioneering-pilot-author-racehorse-trainer-about-1935-image369065261.html.

Page 181: Dr. Joycelyn Elders
Unknown photographer, *Joycelyn Elders,* former U.S. Surgeon General, circa 1993, photograph, National Institutes of Health, via https://en.wikipedia.org/wiki/Joycelyn_Elders.

Page 185: Sybil Ludington
Unknown artist, *Portrait of Sybil Ludington,* unknown date, painting, Heroes, Heroines, and History. https://www.hhhistory.com/2022/08/sybil-ludingtons-revolutionary-midnight.html.

Page 189: Edith Wilson
Harris & Ewing, *Edith Bolling Galt Wilson, full-length portrait, standing, facing front, hands behind waist,* 1913, photograph, Prints and Photographs Division, Library of Congress, digital ID cph.3b39074, https://loc.gov/pictures/resource/ds.16872/.

The Keepers of the Soul:
Page 195: Edna Lewis
John T. Hill, *Photo of Edna Lewis,* 1983, photograph, National Portrait Gallery, Smithsonian Institution; courtesy of National Portrait Gallery Office of Rights and Reproductions, Object Number NPG.2019.119. https://npg.si.edu/object/npg_NPG.2019.119?destination=node/63231%3Fedan_q%3Dedna%2520lewis.

Page 199: Florence Price

G. Nelidoff, *Portrait of Florence Price looking to the side,* unknown date, photograph, courtesy of University of Arkansas Libraries Special Collections, Location MC 988, Box 1, Folder 12, Item 1, https://digitalcollections.uark.edu/digital/collection/p17212coll3/id/23/rec/6.

Page 203: Jarena Lee

P.S. Duval and A. Huffy, *Portrait of Jarena Lee,* circa 1844, lithograph, in Religious Experience and Journal of Mrs. Jarena Lee (self-published, 1849), Harvard College Library, via https://archive.org/details/religiousexperi00leegoog/page/n6/mode/2up.

Page 207: Edith Maude Eaton (aka Sui Sin Far)

Unknown photographer, *Edith Maude Eaton (aka Sui Sin Far),* unknown date, photograph, private collection of Diana Birchall, granddaughter of Winnifred Eaton, via https://en.wikipedia.org/wiki/Sui_Sin_Far.

Page 211: Naomi Long Madgett

Unknown photographer, *Naomi Long Madgett,* 1943, photograph, Private collection of Naomi Long Madgett Estate, courtesy of the Naomi Long Madgett Estate and David Schock, via https://www.nytimes.com/2020/12/04/books/naomi-long-madgett-dead.html.

Page 215: Hettie Anderson

Norman L. Coe Studio, *Hettie Anderson,* circa mid-1890s, photograph, Norman L. Coe Studio, via https://www.nytimes.com/2021/08/12/obituaries/hettie-anderson-overlooked.html.

Page 219: Emma Rowena "Grandma" Gatewood

Unknown photographer, *Emma Gatewood,* unknown date, photograph, private collection of Emma Gatewood, via https://en.wikipedia.org/wiki/Grandma_Gatewood.

Page 223: Sarah Josepha Hale

James Reid Lambdin, *Portrait of Sarah Josepha Hale,* circa 1831, painting, Richards Free Library, Newport, New Hampshire, via https://en.wikipedia.org/wiki/Sarah_Josepha_Hale.

Page 227: Phillis Wheatley

Unknown author, *Portrait of Phillis Wheatley,* 1834, illustration, in Memoir and Poems of Phillis Wheatley, a Native African and a Slave. Dedicated to the Friends of the Africans (Geo. W. Light, 1834), via https://docsouth.unc.edu/neh/wheatley/menu.html.

www.ingramcontent.com/pod-product-compliance
Lightning Source LLC
Chambersburg PA
CBHW041534120626
46551CB00019B/2686